New Kittredge Shakespeare

William Shakespeare

MUCH ADO ABOUT NOTHING

New Kittredge Shakespeare

William Shakespeare

MUCH ADO ABOUT NOTHING

Editor
Peter Kanelos
Loyola University

Series Editor
James H. Lake
Louisiana State University,
Shreveport

focus an imprint of
Hackett Publishing Company, Inc.
Indianapolis/Cambridge

Edited by George Lyman Kittredge.
Used with permission from the heirs to the Kittredge estate.
New material by Peter Kanelos used with permission.

Cover Design by Guy Wetherbee | Elk Amino Design, New England | elkaminodesign.com

Cover illustration: Illustration for a scene in 'Much Ado About Nothing', c. 1900 (color litho), Printz, Christian August (1819-67) Private Collection/Archives Charmet/The Bridgman Art Library International

ISBN: 978-1-58510-267-9
ISBN 10: 1-58510-267-9
Previously published by Focus Publishing/ R. Pullins Company

Focus an imprint of
Hackett Publishing Company

Hackett Publishing Company, Inc.
P.O. Box 44937
Indianapolis, Indiana 46244-0937

www.hackettpublishing.com

TABLE OF CONTENTS

Publisher's Note

George Lyman Kittredge was one of the foremost American Shakespeare scholars of the 20th century. The New Kittredge Shakespeare, builds on his celebrated scholarship and extensive notes. Each edition contains a new, updated introduction, with comments on contemporary film versions of the play, new and revised notes, including performance notes, an essay on reading the play as performance, plus topics for discussion and an annotated bibliography and filmography. For this an accomplished Shakespeare and film scholar has been commissioned to modernize each volume.

The series focuses on understanding the language and allusions in the play as well as encountering Shakespeare as performance. The audience ranges from students at all levels, as well as to readers interested in encountering the text in the context of performance on stage or film.

Ron Pullins, Publisher
Newburyport, 2009

INTRODUCTION TO THE KITTREDGE EDITION

On August 4, 1600, the Stationers' Register records that "The commedie of muche A doo about nothing" (along with "As you like yt," "Henry the ffift," and "Euery man in his humor") is "to be staied." The meaning of this note is far from clear. Perhaps the actors, in accordance with their usual policy, were attempting to block publication. On August 23, however, *Much Ado about Nothing* was regularly entered in the Register by Andrew Wyse and William Aspley.[1] Their edition (in quarto) came out before the end of the year.[2] On this Quarto of 1600 is based the text of the present edition. In setting up the First Folio—which is less accurate than the Quarto, but supplies a number of corrections—the printers must have used a copy of the Quarto that had served as a prompt book and contained some manuscript changes, mostly in stage directions and speech headings.[3]

Meres, in the list of Shakespeare's comedies which he gives in his *Palladis Tamia* (1598), does not mention *Much Ado*, but when the Quarto appeared, in 1600, the play had been "sundrie times publikely acted" by the Lord Chamberlain's players (Shakespeare's company), as the title-page informs us. The part of Dogberry was taken by Will Kempe.[4] This is proved by speech headings in the Quarto (4.2). Kempe left the Lord Chamberlain's Company early in 1599. Thus we may confidently fix the date of the play as the winter of 1598–99. Style and meter accord with this date.

The main plot comes from the twenty-second story in Matteo Bandello's *Novelle* (1554), which Shakespeare may have read in the original or in the translation in Volume III of Belleforest's *Histoires Tragiques* (1569). Bandello goes back, somehow, to the Greek romance of *Chæreas and Callirrhoë*, by one Chariton, who lived about

---

1   The Stationers' Register served as a sort of copyright service; all new plays were required to be registered before being published. [P.K.]

2   A quarto was an inexpensive edition of a single play. About half of Shakespeare's plays were printed in quarto form. A folio was a larger, hardbound, costlier book. The First Folio refers to the first complete collection of Shakespeare's plays, published by members of his acting company in 1623 (seven years after Shakespeare's death). [P.K.]

3   A prompt book was the handwritten copy of the play used by an acting company. Actors received only partial copies of a script, limited to their own lines and short cues lines that would tell them when to speak; thus the prompt book was often the only complete copy of a play before it was printed by a publisher. [P.K.]

4   Will Kempe was the principal comic actor of the Lord Chamberlain's Men. [P.K.]

vii

the late fourth or early fifth century; but all this is prehistoric, so far as Shakespeare is concerned.

The merry war of Benedick and Beatrice and the verbal and logical contortions of Dogberry and Verges are Shakespeare's own. Dogberry is foreshadowed by Dull the Constable in *Love's Labour's Lost* (1594), and Elbow reflects him in *Measure for Measure* (1604). He and his associates in the Police Department of Messina are not mere fun-makers. Of course we must laugh at them. We take unstinted delight in remembering that Dogberry is an ass, and we rejoice that Shakespeare has written him down in that capacity. But after all, these Malapropic watchmen are 'vigitant' enough to arrest the right man at the right moment. What more can one ask of any custodians of the public peace? It is Leonato's inevitable haste that cancels the instant effect of their promptitude and thus precipitates the almost tragic catastrophe at Hero's wedding. We, the audience, know the facts and, since we have come to the theatre to witness a comedy, we are not unduly agitated by the crisis. The examination of Borachio follows immediately and Leonato learns the truth.

The titular villain of *Much Ado* is Don John, Don Pedro's bastard brother. Don John is, by nature, a brooding malcontent. He has risen in fruitless rebellion against his legitimate brother and has been forgiven and restored to favor. But he cherishes that resentment which, in the corrupted currents of this world, a pardoned offender so often feels for his pardoner. Then, too, he is bitterly envious of "the most exquisite" Claudio, who has "all the glory of his overthrow" and is now Don Pedro's "right hand." Don John's "spirits toil in frame of villainies." For both plotting and action, however, he is entirely dependent on his henchman Borachio.

Poor Claudio has suffered unmerciful castigation at the hands of modern critics. Swinburne calls him "a pitiful fellow." Andrew Lang declares that "he behaves throughout like the most hateful young cub." Grace Trenery, though less harsh in language, is likewise condemnatory. She styles him "a vain young sentimentalist." The onus of blame rests, obviously, not so much on Claudio's belief in Hero's guilt as on his plan to denounce and reject her at the marriage altar. But let us not forget that Don Pedro agrees heartily with Claudio in this plan and that it is Don Pedro who proclaims as an eyewitness (4.1):

> Upon mine honor,
> Myself, my brother, and this grieved Count
> Did see her, hear her, at that hour last night
> Talk with a ruffian at her chamber window,
> Who hath indeed, most like a liberal villain,
> Confess'd the vile encounters they have had
> A thousand times in secret.

Even her father is convinced, and he takes her swoon as a confession:

> Would the two princes lie? and Claudio lie,
> Who lov'd her so that, speaking of her foulness,
> Wash'd it with tears? Hence from her! let her die.

After all, we must remember that—though the scene at the wedding is Shakespeare's invention—the disgracing of Hero is the essential point in the ancient story, as the King's credulity is the essential point in the legend of Lear. Omit or modify it and we have lost the play.

The merry war between Benedick and Beatrice seems, at first, to be merely an underplot, but it soon becomes inextricable from the whole structure. Indeed, if comparisons were not odious, one might be tempted to agree with those critics who declare that it usurps the position of the main plot. At all events, *Much Ado about Nothing* ends with a dance. It is Benedick who bids the pipers strike up, and we remember that a star danced when Beatrice was born.

Introduction to the Focus Edition

> "In tragedy, the individual is *not reconcilable* with the universe, and the symbol of their opposition is death. In comedy, the individual *is reconcilable* with the universe, and the symbol for their harmony is marriage."
>
> (W.H. Auden)[1]

Looking over the list of plays at the front of the First Folio, the original collected edition of William Shakespeare's dramatic works (1623), we notice something striking: in contrast to the Tragedies, which are named exclusively after distinct persons (*Hamlet, Othello, Romeo and Juliet*), the titles of the Comedies are general, referring to events, phenomena, or character types (*A Midsummer Night's Dream, The Tempest, The Merchant of Venice*). At the heart of Shakespeare's distinction between tragedy and comedy, this difference suggests, is the fate of the individual. Unlike Shakespeare's tragedies, which are focused intensely upon increasingly isolated protagonists, each of whom ends up not only alone, but dead, his comedies are concerned first and foremost with the reunification of splintered couples, families, and societies.

Whether they tell of twins separated in a storm at sea, young lovers kept apart by disapproving elders, or a duke exiled to an uncharted island, Shakespeare's comedies begin with characters who are estranged—by circumstance and/or sentiment—yet who are reconciled by the play's conclusion. The signature force that brings about this resolution is love, that phenomenon which compels selflessness over selfishness. The arena of encounter is that of romantic relationships. Thus all of Shakespeare's comedies end with marriage or the promise of marriage, indicating the renewal of community in the face of divisiveness. In the comic world, love, in due course, is triumphant.

Much Ado About Nothing, as a comedy, is thus concerned with the nature of romantic love: What sparks it? How is it tested? Why does it triumph? *Does* it always triumph? To look at these questions as fully as possible, Shakespeare presents in *Much Ado* parallel tales of romance, each approaching the experience from radically different angles. On the one side, we have two youthful, naïve lovers who are eager to be joined in matrimony; on the other, we have a man and a woman, jaded by their experiences, each resolved to remain alone.

---

1   W.H. Auden, *Lectures on Shakespeare*, ed. Arthur Kirsch (Princeton: Princeton University Press, 2000), 44.

Claudio and Hero are conventional characters taken from well-worn stories of love. In fact, the two are so evidently lifted from romantic tales as to appear almost two-dimensional. He is dashing and heroic, flush with recent success on the battlefield. She is blushing and demure, the highly marriageable daughter of a leading citizen. They agree rashly, perhaps too rashly, to wed. What makes each appear shallow is that they do not—or cannot—attempt to explore their feelings for one another. Their relationship is marked by silence: they barely speak to one another and when they do it is in a whisper that we do not hear. They do not know one another intimately, which at first allows them to fall blindly for each other, but soon leads to their separation. The course of their relationship is interrupted by a stock villain, straight from central casting, Don John, one also "not of many words" (1.1), whose motivation for villainy is as thinly-examined as their love (in fact, Shakespeare strips his explicit motivation—jealousy—found in the sources that he drew upon for his play). The impediment to the love of Hero and Claudio lies outside their relationship; it is, in effect, a plot device.

Shakespeare weaves into this story his own, original tale—Beatrice and Benedick have no known literary predecessors, as Kittredge notes in his introduction to the play. Shakespeare crafts these two characters to be critics of love and all its conventions. They resist stubbornly those feelings that Hero and Claudio give so readily in to. At the play's opening, Benedick is a noted womanizer, a "tyrant to their sex," who, convinced that women cannot remain faithful, is resolved to remain single:

> That a woman conceived me, I thank her; that she brought me up, I likewise give her most humble thanks; but that I will have a rechate winded in my forehead, or hang my bugle in an invisible baldrick, all women shall pardon me.[2] Because I will not do them the wrong to mistrust any, I will do myself the right to trust none; and the fine is (for the which I may go the finer), I will live a bachelor.

Beatrice, likewise, is determined to live unwed, unwilling to place herself under the authority of a husband. When her uncle, Leonato, expresses his hope that she be married some day, Beatrice retorts:

> Not till God make men of some other metal than earth. Would it not grieve a woman to be overmaster'd with a piece of valiant dust? to make an account of her life to a clod of wayward marl? No, uncle, I'll none. Adam's sons are my brethren, and truly I hold it a sin to match in my kindred.

Both Benedick and Beatrice appear to be evading marriage to retain their liberty, and we find their unconventional attitude towards relationships both entertaining and refreshing. Leonato refers to their sparring as a "merry war," and

---

2   "Rechate" and "bugle" refer to horns; horns were associated with being cuckolded. [P.K.]

in stark contrast to the real war that has just ended, this one, an idle amusement, appears to be without victims.

Yet as much as Benedick and Beatrice claim to be repelled by the idea of love, it is obvious that they are attracted to one another. While Claudio and Hero rarely address one another, Benedick can hardly stop talking to or about Beatrice; she in turn uses every opportunity to turn the conversation towards him. Howsoever ardently Benedick and Beatrice disavow love and/or each other (which, we are quick to understand, amounts to the same thing), it is clear to all around them that the impediments to their love are internal, bound to their personal histories, reputations and egos. In this way, Shakespeare creates a pair of lovers who seem to us more "real"—in our own experience, the barriers to love are not mustachioed villains, but rather insecurity and misunderstanding. These are the sorts of obstacles that must be overcome if love is to triumph.

The title of the play indicates what is standing in the way of love and how it might be amended. To the Elizabethan ear, "nothing" sounded very close to "noting." Taking advantage of this near pun, *Much Ado About Nothing* is a play in which there is much ado about *noting*: characters are constantly observing, eavesdropping, and spying. Sometimes the information they gather is interpreted correctly, but most often it is distorted and misunderstood: Don John mistakenly thinks that he hears Don Pedro wooing Hero for himself and passes on this information to Claudio; both Beatrice and Benedick listen in on their friends, who pretend that they do not know that they are being observed; Don John orchestrates a false scene in which Claudio is led to believe that Hero is entertaining another man in her room at night; and so forth. The overall effect of these episodes is to impress upon us that we understand the world only superficially and that we should be skeptical about what we see and hear, seeking confirmation before making assumptions. Moreover, there is another association with "nothing" that ties together the play's concerns. In Shakespeare's day, "nothing" was also bawdy slang for, as Hamlet terms it, what "lie[s] between a maid's legs" (*Hamlet* 3.2). In *Much Ado*, the multiple meanings of nothing/noting are entangled, and therein lies the problem – the "noting" of the male characters (their late-night spying) of "nothing" (Hero's supposed sexual liaison) should reveal to them that "nothing" is going on (she is in fact a virgin and utterly devoted). Yet it does not, and the play asks us why this is the case.

One of the great ironies of *Much Ado About Nothing* is that while women are consistently maligned for being unfaithful, it is the *men* who are inconstant. Their allegiances, beginning with Don John turning against his own brother in the war that has just come to an end, are ever-shifting. Beatrice derides Benedick for having a new best friend every week and from jumping from woman to woman, and he does not contradict her. Claudio brutally drops Hero without allowing that *he* might be in the wrong. In a moment of male bonding, Don Pedro, Leonato, and Claudio (with Benedick listening in), ask for a song (2.3):

> Sigh no more, ladies, sigh no more!
> Men were deceivers ever,

> One foot in sea, and one on shore;
> To one thing constant never
> Then sigh not so,
> But let them go,
> And be you blithe and bonny,
> Converting all your sounds of woe
> Into Hey nonny, nonny.

The lyrics are clear—men are not trustworthy, women should be wary—but the men are not listening, not, as it were, noting the notes. They continue on with their conversation without pause or a second thought.

The problem, it seems, is not simply that men are "constant never," but rather that they are not self-aware. They do not recognize their own faults, and, worse, impute those faults upon others. In the world of *Much Ado*, men are obsessed with "honor," that is, with upholding their own sense of self-worth, in accord with male codes of conduct ("men" and its derivative forms are, in fact, the most frequent words in this play). Concern for one's own standing above all else is a radical form of self-centeredness, and, in the world of Shakespeare's plays, a direct path to a tragic denouement. For all to end well, the principal male characters must divest themselves of their selfishness.

The names of the lead female characters indicate to us how this process will unfold. "Hero" was a byword for faithfulness in the Renaissance. In the legend of Hero and Leander (which Christopher Marlowe had updated prior to Shakespeare's play in a popular narrative poem), Hero proves her fidelity to her beloved, Leander, by lighting a lamp in her tower window each evening so that he can swim across the Hellespont to be with her; when he drowns while making his way to her one night, she throws herself into the channel, unable to live without him. In *Much Ado*, Claudio must learn that his Hero does in fact live up to her name and that *he* is the inconstant one (of course Shakespeare, significantly, chooses not to name *him* Leander).

The name Beatrice is associated with Dante's great work, *The Divine Comedy*.[3] Based on Beatrice Portinari, she is Dante's ideal woman, and in his poem leads the narrator from Purgatory up through Heaven. The *Oxford English Dictionary* thus defines a "Beatrician" experience as "the recovery (in respect to one human being) of that vision of reality which would have been common to all men in respect to all things if Man had never fallen." Given that Benedick's name translates as "one who is blessed," it is clear that he will, as will Claudio, be elevated by the grace of the woman that he loves.

---

3   We are not certain that Shakespeare read the *Divine Comedy*, but since Dante's work was one of the most important literary influences on Renaissance culture, it is probable that one as widely-read as Shakespeare would have had at least secondary familiarity with the figure of Beatrice.

Generally, Beatrice and Benedick are seen as equally resistant to love, and it is often played this way in the theater. She has the first volley, as she puts down Benedick even before he has arrived, impugning him as "Signor Mountanto" (in Kittredge's note, "an upright blow or thrust in fencing," but also implying a social climber, "mount onto," or even a sexual opportunist). They are both seemingly eager combatants in the merry war. Yet a small detail slips in that provides depth of perspective: we learn that Beatrice once gave Benedick her heart and that he broke it.[4] Her resistance to love, and from loving Benedick in particular, comes from the experience of rejection and pain. Yet it is through suffering that she has learned what it is to love, and it is her charge to tutor Benedick.

In the gulling scenes, Beatrice and Benedick are tricked into recognizing their affections in almost identical ways. But the nature of their separate responses indicates that they are not yet equally primed to love. After hearing his friends discuss how Beatrice secretly adores him, Benedick *decides* that her love must be requited, even if he will be mocked for his decision (2.3):

> I may chance have some odd quirks and remnants of wit broken
> on me because I have railed so long against marriage. But doth
> not the appetite alter? A man loves the meat in his youth that he
> cannot endure in his age. Shall quips and sentences and these
> paper bullets of the brain awe a man from the career of his
> humor? No, the world must be peopled. When I said I would die
> a bachelor, I did not think I should live till I were married.

His language is logical, calculating, and his contention—the world must, after all, be peopled—is sound. It is also one of the least romantic confessions of love that one could imagine. Tellingly, it is in prose, which, for Shakespeare, is the vehicle for reasoned thought (and, conspicuously, humor). Beneath Benedick's speech reside authentic feelings; but he is still hiding behind the mask of rational argument. He is leading himself to believe, as his pride perhaps dictates, that although he is prepared to plunge into unfamiliar territory, he still retains a sense of control.

In stark contrast is Beatrice's reaction to hearing her friends claim that Benedick loves her, but that her shrewish nature has kept him at bay (3.1):

> What fire is in mine ears? Can this be true?
> Stand I condemn'd for pride and scorn so much?
> Contempt, farewell! and maiden pride, adieu!
> No glory lives behind the back of such.
> And, Benedick, love on; I will require thee,
> Taming my wild heart to thy loving hand.
> If thou dost love, my kindness shall incite thee

---

4   When Leonato jokingly says to Beatrice that she has lost Benedick's heart, she replies with surprising candor: "Indeed, my lord, he lent it me awhile, and I gave him use for it—a double heart for his single one. Marry, once before he won it of me with false dice; therefore your Grace may well say I have lost it" (2.1).

> To bind our loves up in a holy band;
> For others say thou dost deserve, and I
> Believe it better than reportingly.

She responds in rhymed verse, a shortened sonnet in fact, in language that registers her heightened emotions and sense of transport. More critically, she expresses her willingness to submit to him. Love, she understands, is not concerned with maintaining control and dominance, but rather with yielding one's will to the beloved; if this is *mutually* accomplished the foundation for love is set.

Thus the lesson that Beatrice teaches Benedick is one of surrender. In the wedding scene (4.1), Hero is accused publicly by Claudio, and the men close ranks around him, certain that his honor has been impugned by her transgression. Yet Benedick separates himself from the male clique; watching Beatrice's deeply empathetic response to Hero's plight, he is moved to declare his love to her—and his love is immediately tested. *Much Ado* makes an emotional pivot when Beatrice demands that Benedick, "Kill Claudio." Benedick, a fighter turned lover, is now asked once again to be a fighter. Moreover, he is asked to stand up to and against the code of male honor that has up to this point directed his own behavior. He is asked to put the honor of Hero above this code, above his allegiance to his comrades, above, even, his bonds of friendship. He is asked, in essence, to make all other concerns subordinate to the wishes of the woman he loves. At first, he falters: to Beatrice's request to kill Claudio, he responds, "Ha! Not for the wide world!" But as he witnesses Beatrice's fierce devotion to her cousin—"O God, that I were a man! I would eat his heart in the market place"—he transforms. His feelings for Beatrice make her a sort of emotional conduit for him—men, in their selfishness, *do* eat the hearts of women. A professed tyrant to their sex now sees such tyranny from the outside. In putting the honor of Hero above his own inclinations—that is, in trusting the will of Beatrice unconditionally—Benedick comes to understand honor differently. Rather than putting himself first, he commits to action that will upend his friendships, compromise his standing, and even endanger his life, all for the benefit of another. And he does so ultimately not for Hero, but for Beatrice.

Claudio also learns a lesson by mourning for Hero. The second time in *Much Ado* that a song is sung concerning fidelity and its attendant woe, the men *are* listening (5.3):

> Pardon, goddess of the night,
> Those that slew thy virgin knight;
> For the which, with songs of woe,
> Round about her tomb they go.

They are contrite, singing "songs of woe," and Don Pedro subtly registers their new perspective: he tells them that with the coming of dawn it is time to leave Hero's tomb, as "the wolves have preyed." Those who have just *prayed* at Hero's monument are finally recognized for what they are, or have been: wolves that have *preyed*. To pay penance, Claudio turns his will over to Hero's father, Leonato, and agrees to marry his "niece." Although Claudio and Hero are ultimately reconciled, it is an odd thing to prove one's devotion by giving over one's hand in marriage to a third party. Thus Claudio's conversion seems less satisfying – perhaps because Shakespeare wanted it to be so.

As Auden remarked, the marriages at the end of Shakespeare's comedies signify reconciliation, not just for the characters who are to be wed, but for the community as a whole. Yet what makes *Much Ado About Nothing*, like all of Shakespeare's comedies, so rich, is that it resists simplicity and clarity at its conclusion. Don John is still waiting in the wings to be punished. Hero's forgiveness of Claudio is unsettling. And Beatrice and Benedick, who have charmed us and each other with their witty words, stop their mouths with a kiss—causing us to wonder whether their marriage will have the same charge as their unorthodox courtship.

Shakespeare's tragedies end in death—but the pathways that the characters blaze towards their fall leave behind a residue of memorable glory: as Juliet says of Romeo: "when he shall die, /Take him and cut him out in little stars, / And he will make the face of heaven so fine / That all the world will be in love with night" (*Romeo and Juliet* 3.2). In the comedies, the things that make the principal characters so remarkable and enjoyable, what make them stand out and apart from the general population, must be suppressed. The comedies glory in the rocky friction of romance, not the sustained smoothness of love. That which that made characters distinct must ultimately dissolve as society reconstitutes itself. Thus *Much Ado About Nothing* ends with a dance—a sign of harmony, yet also a sign that the time has come for all to remain in step together.

Much Ado About Nothing in Performance

The record of performance of Shakespeare's plays during his lifetime is scant and uneven. For most, we know only loosely when they were written or first staged. Thus even though the first quarto edition of *Much Ado About Nothing* (1600) announces on its title page, as Kittredge notes, that the play had been "sundrie times publikely acted"—and there is no reason to doubt that this was true—the earliest direct documentation of a performance of *Much Ado* is found near the end of Shakespeare's career, when the play, listed as "Benedicte and Betteris," was performed along with several others in 1613 for the wedding festivities surrounding the marriage of Princess Elizabeth, daughter to King James I.[5]

Despite this slim account, it is clear from other cultural references that *Much Ado* was a popular play from the start and that the "merry war" was seen to be the central feature of the action. In fact, King Charles I (brother to Princess Elizabeth) would later amend the play's title in his own copy of the Second Folio (1632) to "Benedik and Betrice." The early popularity of this couple, and of *Much Ado*, is

---

5   In the accounts of the Lord Chamberlain a payment was made on 20 May 1613 to Shakespeare's company for "presenting before the Princess highness the Lady Elizabeth and the Prince Pallatyne Elector fowerteene severall playes," including "Benedicte and Betteris." See E. K. Chambers, *The Elizabethan Stage*, 4 vol. (Oxford: Clarendon Press, 1923), 2:343.

further attested to in verse by Leonard Digges in his edition of Shakespeare's *Poems* (1640): "let but Beatrice / And Benedick be seene, loe in a trice, / The Cockpit, Galleries, Boxes, all are full."[6] Apparently a commercial and comic success in Shakespeare's day, Beatrice and Benedick have remained popular figures ever since, inspiring countless other sparring couples in the theater and, later, on film.

By 1642, all playhouses in England had been shut down following a Puritan-led revolt against the monarchy and the subsequent imposition of a rigid code of public morality. Theaters were seen as places of ill repute, in part because they featured men dressed as women (all female roles were played by boy actors). They would remain closed until 1660, when Charles II, the son of the deposed and beheaded Charles I, returned from exile and resumed his authority. By this time, Shakespeare's plays were over half-a-century old and although he remained an important playwright, acting companies took great liberties in adapting his works to suit the tastes of contemporary audiences.

Thus in 1662 William Davenant lifted the ever-popular Beatrice and Benedick from *Much Ado* and transported them to a new play, *Law Against Lovers*, the plot of which was taken from Shakespeare's *Measure for Measure*. Benedick is made the brother of Angelo (from *Measure*), and Beatrice is Angelo's ward (and also an heiress). Hero and Claudio are absent, possibly accounted for by the Restoration's distaste for seemingly sentimental love stories. Samuel Pepys, the inveterate diarist, saw the play and found it to his liking, especially the singing and dancing of Beatrice's younger sister, Viola. Davenant's use of four important female roles highlighted another significant development in the life of *Much Ado* (and in English theater)— the introduction of female actors to the stage (first introduced in December 1660). Having spent his youth in Paris, where women had long been actors, King Charles II repealed the legal statutes that prohibited women from acting on the English stage.[7] Thus Beatrice and Benedick squared off literally as woman versus man for the first time ever in Davenant's production, even if transported from their original play.

Much Ado was revived at Lincoln's Inn in 1721, and it is possible that this was the first time that a version approximating Shakespeare's original had been staged in a century. Yet it would fall to David Garrick, the most acclaimed actor of his day, to bring *Much Ado About Nothing* back to prominence. Garrick was the single figure most responsible for transforming Shakespeare from a renowned Elizabethan playwright to the revered "national poet" of England; he first caught the public's attention as Richard III, and in 1769 he produced the Jubilee, a massive celebration held in Stratford-upon-Avon honoring Shakespeare and his work. Garrick's *Much Ado* was a great crowd-pleaser and Benedick was his most successful comic role. From 1748, Garrick played the part every year, until his retirement in 1776. During this tenure, several successive Beatrices played opposite him. Garrick's productions,

---

6   Preface to the 1640 edition of Shakespeare's poems, in Chambers, 2:233.

7   The film, *Stage Beauty* (2004), directed by Richard Eyre, dramatizes this critical moment in English theater history.

rapidly-paced, animated, and sharp, highlighted the badinage between Beatrice and Benedick, both figures of wit and fashion, angling for social superiority.

In the early nineteenth century, with a rising cultural emphasis on "feeling" and "sensibility," Beatrice and Benedick, in addition to being presented as characters of sharp wit, were also played with greater emotional depth. The actor-manager Charles Kemble focused on the psychological underpinnings of the two, finding a suppressed attraction even from the start. Benedick was a man of honor, Beatrice a character of substantial empathy. The more serious aspects of the play were also focused upon to the extent that William Hazlitt suggested that "Hero was the principal figure," and Beatrice and Benedick "the principal *comic* characters."[8] In the church scene (4.1), when Hero collapses after being indicted by Claudio, Kemble rushed to catch her from the one side, while Beatrice stayed her from the other, the lovers' first embrace therefore coming as they mutually support the falsely accused woman. Their instinctual empathy overcomes their caustic wit, bringing them together at last.

In the later nineteenth century, with the advent of improved indoor lighting and sophisticated stage machinery, we find an increasing grandiosity in Shakespearean productions. Attending a Shakespearean play, one could expect to find "a series of convincing and romantic pictures, with which the characters would move in picturesque and appropriate costumes. The events of the play would unfold in harmonious and well-planned succession, each movement of the plot climaxing in a striking tableau and the whole welded together with orchestral music."[9] Spectacle began to take precedence over characterization and narrative. Sir Henry Irving's *Much Ado*, which ran for 212 performances, was acclaimed as much for its lavish sets as it was for the acting of Irving and his opposite, Ellen Terry. A painting by Forbes-Robertson of the wedding scene illustrates how the "...production featured an Italian cathedral with stained-glass windows and statues of saints, thirty-foot-high pillars, and a canopied roof of crimson plush from which hung golden lamps. The floor was covered with vases of flower, and flaming candles rose to a height of eighteen feet."[10] The effect was dazzling, but for some critics the play suffered from such distractions.

Towards the turn of the twentieth century, directors began to move away from the pictorialist approach. The productions of William Poel, including *Much Ado About Nothing* in 1904, attempted to recreate the theatrical conventions of the Renaissance. His actors performed on a facsimile of an Elizabethan stage, wore costumes suggesting the late-sixteenth and early-seventeenth centuries, and were accompanied by early modern music played on period instruments. More

---

8   In John F. Cox, ed. *Shakespeare in Production: Much Ado About Nothing* (Cambridge: Cambridge University Press, 1997), 24.

9   Russell Jackson in *The Oxford Illustrated History of Shakespeare on Stage*, eds. Jonathan Bate and Russell Jackson (Oxford: Oxford University Press, 2001), 114.

10   Jeffrey Kahan in *Shakespeare in Performance: Much Ado About Nothing* (London: Methuen, 2007), 8.

importantly, Poel reintroduced certain Elizabethan stage practices, including fluid scene changes, the minimal use of stage properties and scenery, and language spoken trippingly on the tongue. Some saw Poel's endeavors as antiquarian, but others began to adopt the principles of leaner, cleaner Shakespeare in response to the baroque extravagance of Victorian and Edwardian productions.

Edward Gordon Craig, like Poel, adhered to the principle of simplicity in production, but in a more stylized fashion, finding a middle ground between the attempt to create the illusion of reality and the reversion to historically-specific practices. His staging of the church scene—a backdrop of folded curtains suggesting columns, a stream of light from on high suggesting a stained-glass window—was much acclaimed for its expressionistic, emotive effect. His approach was approved of by George Bernard Shaw, who commented, "we are less conscious of artificiality of the stage when a few well-understood conventions, adroitly handled, are substituted for attempts at impossible scenic verisimilitude."[11] Although productions of great extravagance continued to be mounted—most conspicuously those of Herbert Beerbohm Tree, who staged detailed Sicilian landscapes and Italianate gardens replete with live larks singing in his 1905 production at His Majesty's Theatre—the rise of film as a medium, which could marshal much greater illusionistic resources, had the effect of pushing stage plays towards the impressionistic and conceptual.

Sir John Gielgud directed *Much Ado* at Stratford in 1949 and set the standard for productions of the middle of the twentieth century. Taking the role of Benedick in revivals (1950, 1952, 1955) Gielgud played opposite Diana Wynyard, Peggy Ashcroft and Margaret Leighton. He describes in his memoir, *Stage Directions*, how his conception of Benedick evolved over time from a foppish comic figure, decked out in ridiculous hats, to a brusque military man, who is transformed by Beatrice's tears after the wedding debacle.[12] Although Gielgud's backdrop was pure Renaissance, with tones of Boccaccio, the trend in the twentieth century was to seek out less orthodox settings that would highlight the social dynamics of the play.

With the rise of feminism and other forms of social criticism, the focus in *Much Ado* began to shift away from the merry war and to settle more upon a world which could produce double standards in sexual morality and grave disparities in social class. Franco Zeffirelli's production for the National Theatre (1965) placed the action in nineteenth-century Sicily, evoking Mafia codes of *omertà* and honor-killings, and presenting, in accord with the spirit of the day, a sexually-charged atmosphere. John Barton set *Much Ado* in the India of the British Empire for the Royal Shakespeare Company (1976), suggesting complex layers of class stratification and racial segregation, with both Claudio and Don John as blithe imperialists and Dogberry and the Watch as turbaned Sikhs. More recent productions have upended expectations for *Much Ado* even further. In a radical gender reversal on the "reconstructed" Globe stage in London, Tamara Harvey directed an entirely female

11   Cox, 48.

12   John Gielguld, *Stage Directions* (Westport, CT: Greenwood Press, 1979).

cast in 2004, turning on its head the same-gender casting of Shakespeare's original production.

Much Ado About Nothing on Screen

Even though Beatrice and Benedick have provided the template for countless sparring romantic couples on the Hollywood screen, there have been remarkably few feature films made of *Much Ado About Nothing*. In fact, following a lost 1913 silent film which may have been an adaptation of Shakespeare's *Much Ado* (or may have simply used its title for an unrelated story), sixty years would pass before audiences would see a major English-language version broadcast on television – and it would take a full twenty more years for *Much Ado* to receive its debut in the cinema.

What began as a Public Theater stage production of *Much Ado* for the New York Shakespeare Festival, directed by Joseph Papp, was adapted for film by A.J Antoon. Aired in 1973, this televised performance, it was claimed, was seen by more people in that single broadcast than had seen the play in its entire history on stage. Antoon's *Much Ado* was essentially a recording of the original theatrical production, retaining the invisible "fourth-wall" orientation and using filmic effects only sparingly. In accord with the Public Theater's mandate to "Americanize" Shakespeare, the play is set at the close of Teddy Roosevelt's Spanish-American War. The elements of a sentimentalized small-town America are all in place: panama hats, gazebos, banjos, and barber shops. With Sam Waterston as Benedick and Kathleen Widdoes as Beatrice, the production is lyrical, even elegiac, in its incarnation of a lost time and place. Leisurely paced and sweetly discordant rather than biting, the film suggest that love is indeed a "merry war." Don John, fumbling and foppish, is never a creditable threat. Dogberry and crew chase the malefactors about in a comic sequence recalling the antics of the Keystone Cops. The darkest moment comes when Claudio and Don Pedro mourn Hero in the churchyard in the pouring rain, surrounded by a large crowd sheltered beneath black umbrellas; yet the monument on her gravesite, a dimpled statue of Cupid, suggests that love is still to be found in the world. The shadows are soon dispersed when Claudio is introduced to his "new" bride, riding with several other veiled ladies on a carousel.

From 1978-1984, the BBC embarked on an ambitious project to film and televise all of Shakespeare's plays. The quality and critical reception of these productions varied greatly. For the most part, they are rather staid and conservative, typically employing Renaissance costumes and exclusively British actors. *Much Ado* was one of the last of these to be presented to the public, in part because the BBC's first attempt to film the play was abandoned for undisclosed reasons. The second effort, directed by Stuart Burge, was televised in 1984. Although more filmic than Antoon's *Much Ado*, its simple painted backdrops and sparing use of music create the atmosphere of a theatrical production. The first scene is set in the courtyard of an Italian palazzo, and the remainder of the action moves between orchards and halls of Leonato's grand house, decorated with statues and pictures of lions, in reference to his name. The classically-trained cast, led by Cherie Lunghi (Beatrice), Robert

Lindsay (Benedick) and Jon Finch (Don Pedro) is superb, serving Shakespeare's uncut text with clear and sensitive delivery of the language. Beatrice and Benedick, who begin the play with evident antipathy for one another, are quite serious in their aversion to love, which makes their conversion all the more remarkable.

Although the twentieth century would nearly draw to a close before *Much Ado About Nothing* would make it to the big screen, when it finally did, it proved remarkably successful, both commercially and critically. Kenneth Branagh's *Much Ado* (1993) was unabashedly populist, aimed at bringing Shakespeare's play to the widest audience possible, while remaining faithful to the language and spirit of the original. To these ends, Branagh attempted to achieve a synthesis of Hollywood and Shakespeare. His film had a large budget (at least in terms of Shakespearean projects) and thus availed itself of the full array of cinematic resources. This is most evident in the setting—the film was shot on the grounds of a Tuscan villa and is appareled gorgeously. Branagh's synthetic approach is most conspicuous in his choice of a cast: "the challenge was to find experienced Shakespearean actors who were unpracticed on screen and team them with highly experienced film actors who were much less familiar with Shakespeare. Different accents, different looks. An excitement borne out of complementary styles and approaches would produce a Shakespeare film that belonged to the world."[13] Thus a slate of British stage actors, culled mostly from Branagh's own Renaissance Theatre Company—Emma Thompson, Brian Blessed, Richard Biers—was matched with established Hollywood film stars— Denzel Washington, Keanu Reeves, Michael Keaton—as well as up-and-coming screen actors, such as Kate Beckinsale. Although a few of the performances were panned (most notably Keaton's Dogberry, who owed more to Beetlejuice than Shakespeare's comic constable), the film proved lively and accessible. Branagh's Benedick is crisp and cavalier, his railing against love clearly out of synch with the festive spirit in Messina. Yet his caustic wit hides beneath it a deep emotional need; he transforms so quickly, so completely into a lover, that it is clear that Beatrice had always held a place in his heart. The shots following the two gulling scenes—cutting between Benedick splashing joyfully in a fountain and Beatrice blissfully swinging, while a full orchestra renders their love audible—argue, against the text, that their separate paths towards love are not only parallel, but a bit shallow. Yet their scene together immediately following Claudio's humiliating rejection of Hero, shot in a tiny chapel, is so painfully sincere that we can see through Branagh and Thompson how fully dimensional these characters truly are.

The BBC produced four adaptations of Shakespearean plays for television as part of the *Shakespeare Retold* series, including *Much Ado About Nothing* (2005). All four were modernized, both in setting and language, following Shakespeare's originals only loosely. Beatrice and Benedick are newscasters on the "Wessex Tonight" program, Hero is a meteorologist, her father, Leonard, the producer, and

---

13   Kenneth Branagh, *Much Ado About Nothing: Screenplay, Introduction and Notes on the Making of a Movie* (New York: W.W. Norton & Co., 1993), x.

Emma Thompson, as Beatrice, and Kenneth Branagh, as Benedick. (Branagh 1993)

Mr. "Berry" is the overzealous security guard. While many of the scenes parallel Shakespeare's original, the ending of the film is radically different. In this version, Don (Don John) is a jealous suitor, a co-worker but who reads Hero's friendly attentions the wrong way. He conspires on his own to ruin her wedding day by faking text messages and photos and convincing Claude to watch as he enters Hero's room the night before. When Hero confronts Don after Claude has rejected her, Don pushes her violently; she injures her head against a post, sending her to the intensive care unit of the hospital on the brink of death. Hero recovers from her injury, but refuses to forgive Claude, offering only the faintest hope that they might reconcile one day. The film concludes with the wedding of Beatrice and Benedick, laughing at the absurdity of finding themselves at the altar as the final shot fades out.

MUCH ADO ABOUT NOTHING

DRAMATIS PERSONAE

Don Pedro, Prince of Arragon.
Don John, his bastard brother.
Claudio, a young lord of Florence.
Benedick, a young lord of Padua.
Leonato, Governor of Messina.
Antonio, an old man, his brother.
Balthasar, attendant on *Don Pedro.*
Borachio,
Conrade, } followers of *Don John* .
Dogberry, a Constable.
Verges, a Headborough.
A Sexton.
A Boy.

Hero, daughter to *Leonato.*
Beatrice, niece to *Leonato.*
Margaret,
Ursula, } waiting gentlewomen attending on *Hero.*

Messengers, Watch, Attendants, &c.

SCENE. *Messina.*

ACT I

SCENE I. [*An orchard before Leonato's house.*]†

Enter Leonato (Governor of Messina), Hero (his Daughter),
and Beatrice (his Niece), with a Messenger.

LEONATO   I learn in this letter that Don Pedro of Arragon comes this night
                     to Messina.

MESSENGER   He is very near by this. He was not three leagues off when I left
                     him.

LEONATO   How many gentlemen have you lost in this action?   5

MESSENGER   But few of any sort, and none of name.

LEONATO   A victory is twice itself when the achiever brings home full
                     numbers. I find here that Don Pedro hath bestowed much honor
                     on a young Florentine called Claudio.   9

MESSENGER   Much deserv'd on his part, and equally rememb'red by Don Pedro
                     He hath borne himself beyond the promise of his age, doing in the
                     figure of a lamb the feats of a lion. He hath indeed better bett'red
                     expectation than you must expect of me to tell you how.

LEONATO   He hath an uncle here in Messina will be very much glad of it.   14

MESSENGER   I have already delivered him letters, and there appears much joy in
                     him; even so much that joy could not show itself modest enough
                     without a badge of bitterness.

LEONATO   Did he break out into tears?

ACT I. SCENE I.
5. **this action:** this recent battle. 6. **sort:** rank —**name:** high reputation. 16–17. **joy could not...
without a badge of bitterness:** joy could not show itself with becoming moderation unless it wore the
sign of sorrow; or, in plain language, unless he had burst into tears, his joy would have been beyond
control. —**modest:** moderate. That tears, though often the result of joy, are the appropriate marks of
sorrow, is an idea that Shakespeare repeats again and again with much variety of expression.

---

†   The opening scene of Much Ado About Nothing can be staged in ways that establish the larger themes
     that a director wishes to amplify. Branagh's film begins with the characters in Messina picnicking on a
     shady hillside, while Beatrice reads to them the lyrics from the song, "Hey, nonny, nonny," as if reading
     from a book of poetry. In the middle of this scene, he cuts to the soldiers returning from war, riding
     into town on horseback in a shot that recalls the classic Western, The Magnificent Seven. When their
     arrival is announced, the women rush to shower and change into white linen dresses, while the soldiers
     leap into pools to bathe before their reception. The overall effect is one of sexually-charged anticipation
     and celebration. Antoon begins his film with the Messenger meeting Leonato, Hero, Antonio, Ursula and
     Margaret on the front porch of a grand Victorian house, while Beatrice swings off to the side, seemingly
     aloof. In Burge's film, the messenger is greeted by Leonato in his Italianate courtyard, accompanied only by
     Hero and Beatrice, who are sitting on the ledge of a fountain; the dynamic is one of familial intimacy. [P.K.]

MESSENGER	In great measure.	19

LEONATO A kind overflow of kindness. There are no faces truer than those that are so wash'd. How much better is it to weep at joy than to joy at weeping!

BEATRICE I pray you, is Signior Mountanto return'd from the wars or no?

MESSENGER I know none of that name, lady. There was none such in the army of any sort.   25

LEONATO What is he that you ask for, niece?

HERO My cousin means Signior Benedick of Padua.

MESSENGER O, he's return'd, and as pleasant as ever he was.

BEATRICE He set up his bills here in Messina and challeng'd Cupid at the flight, and my uncle's fool, reading the challenge, subscrib'd for Cupid and challeng'd him at the birdbolt. I pray you, how many hath he kill'd and eaten in these wars? But how many hath he kill'd? For indeed I promised to eat all of his killing.

LEONATO Faith, niece, you tax Signior Benedick too much; but he'll be meet with you, I doubt it not.   35

MESSENGER He hath done good service, lady, in these wars.

BEATRICE You had musty victual, and he hath holp to eat it. He is a very valiant trencherman; he hath an excellent stomach.

MESSENGER And a good soldier too, lady.

BEATRICE And a good soldier to a lady; but what is he to a lord?   40

MESSENGER A lord to a lord, a man to a man; stuff'd with all honorable virtues.

BEATRICE It is so indeed. He is no less than a stuff'd man; but for the stuffing—well, we are all mortal.   44

LEONATO You must not, sir, mistake my niece. There is a kind of merry war betwixt Signior Benedick and her. They never meet but there's a skirmish of wit between them.

---

20. **kind:** natural. 23. **Signior Mountanto.** *Montanto* or *montant* was a technical term for an upright blow or thrust in fencing. "Mountanto," as in "mount onto," could also suggest a social climber or even a sexual opportunist [P.K.]. 29. **He set up his bills:** He posted his written notices —of the challenge to Cupid. — **challeng'd Cupid at the flight:** challenged Cupid to a contest in which he would defy Cupid's arrows. —**at the flight:** to an archery duel. 30–31.**subscrib'd for Cupid:** signed as Cupid's representative or substitute. —**at the birdbolt:** for a contest with flat-headed arrows, such as were used to shoot birds. 33. **to eat all of his killing.** A proverbial turn of phrase, indicating that none would be killed. 34. **tax:** take to task, censure. 34–35. **be meet with you:** make you an appropriate answer; be a match for your gibes. 37. **holp:** helped. 38. **trencherman:** eater. A *trencher* is a wooden plate or platter. —**stomach:** appetite. 40. **to:** in comparison with; in a contest with. 43. **a stuff'd man:** a mere figure of a man—clothes stuffed to resemble a living being. 43–44. **but for the stuffing…mortal:** but, as to what he's actually made of (what qualities of mind and character he is, as you call it "stuffed with")—well, perhaps he's no worse than the rest of us poor human creatures.

BEATRICE	Alas, he gets nothing by that! In our last conflict four of his five wits went halting off, and now is the whole man govern'd with one; so that if he have wit enough to keep himself warm, let him bear it for a difference between himself and his horse; for it is all the wealth that he hath left to be known a reasonable creature. Who is his companion now? He hath every month a new sworn brother.	
MESSENGER	Is't possible?	55
BEATRICE	Very easily possible. He wears his faith but as the fashion of his hat; it ever changes with the next block.	
MESSENGER	I see, lady, the gentleman is not in your books.	
BEATRICE	No. An he were, I would burn my study. But I pray you, who is his companion? Is there no young squarer now that will make a voyage with him to the devil?	61
MESSENGER	He is most in the company of the right noble Claudio.	
BEATRICE	O Lord, he will hang upon him like a disease! He is sooner caught than the pestilence, and the taker runs presently mad. God help the noble Claudio! If he have caught the Benedick, it will cost him a thousand pound ere 'a be cured.	66
MESSENGER	I will hold friends with you, lady.	
BEATRICE	Do, good friend.	
LEONATO	You will never run mad, niece.	
BEATRICE	No, not till a hot January.	70
MESSENGER	Don Pedro is approach'd.	

Enter Don Pedro, Claudio, Benedick, Balthasar, and John the Bastard.‡

48–49. **his five wits.** The five wits (mental faculties) are common wit, imagination, fantasy, estimation, and memory. —**halting:** limping. —**with:** by. 50. **wit enough to keep himself warm.** A proverbial synonym for "the least particle of intelligence." 50–51. **let him bear it for a difference:** let him keep that fact as a mark in his coat of arms. A *difference* is a slight variation in such a coat, usually indicating that one belongs to a younger branch of the family. 51–52. **for it…creature:** for that modicum of intelligence is all that he has in the way of wits to show that he is a reasonable creature and not a mere dumb animal. The *horse* often serves as an example of stupidity. 53–54. **sworn brother:** In medieval times friends would often take a solemn oath to stand by each other in life and death as faithfully as if they were brothers indeed. 57. **block:** fashion. 58. **in your books:** in your good books; in your favor; one of your friends. In her reply Beatrice, for the jest's sake, takes the words in their literal sense. 59. **An:** if. 60. **squarer:** quarrelsome fellow—always "squaring off" for a fight. 64. **presently:** instantly. 66. **'a:** he. 67. **I will hold friends with you:** The speaker indicates that he wishes to keep on friendly terms with a lady who has such a sharp tongue. 69. **You will never run mad:** Whoever may run mad as the result of accepting Benedick as a friend, *you* certainly will not.

---

‡   In Antoon's film, a brass marching band escorts the returning soldiers through crowded streets to a gazebo at the center of the town square, where they are greeted by Leonato. [P.K.]

Beatrice and Benedick square off as rival news anchors in the *Shakespeare Retold* adaptation of *Much Ado About Nothing*, produced by the BBC. (2005)

DON PEDRO	Good Signior Leonato, are you come to meet your trouble? The fashion of the world is to avoid cost, and you encounter it.
LEONATO	Never came trouble to my house in the likeness of your Grace; for trouble being gone, comfort should remain; but when you depart from me, sorrow abides and happiness takes his leave. 76
DON PEDRO	You embrace your charge too willingly. I think this is your daughter.
LEONATO	Her mother hath many times told me so.
BENEDICK	Were you in doubt, sir, that you ask'd her? 80
LEONATO	Signior Benedick, no; for then were you a child.
DON PEDRO	You have it full, Benedick. We may guess by this what you are, being a man. Truly the lady fathers herself. Be happy, lady; for you are like an honorable father.
BENEDICK	If Signior Leonato be her father, she would not have his head 85 on her shoulders for all Messina, as like him as she is.
BEATRICE	I wonder that you will still be talking, Signior Benedick. Nobody marks you.

---

72. **your trouble:** It was the old fashion for a guest to dwell upon the trouble he gave his host. 73. **cost:** expense. 77. **charge:** burden of expense and trouble. 82. **You have it full:** That's a good hit for you! You have had your answer! 83. **fathers herself:** proves by her likeness to her father that she is his child. 85. **his head:** his head with its white hair and beard. Benedick finds it amusing to think of Hero as closely resembling her old father.

BENEDICK	What, my dear Lady Disdain! are you yet living?
BEATRICE	Is it possible Disdain should die while she hath such meet food 90 to feed it as Signior Benedick? Courtesy itself must convert to disdain if you come in her presence.
BENEDICK	Then is courtesy a turncoat. But it is certain I am loved of all ladies, only you excepted; and I would I could find in my heart that I had not a hard heart, for truly I love none. 95
BEATRICE	A dear happiness to women! They would else have been troubled with a pernicious suitor. I thank God and my cold blood, I am of your humor for that. I had rather hear my dog bark at a crow than a man swear he loves me.
BENEDICK	God keep your ladyship still in that mind! So some gentleman 101 or other shall scape a predestinate scratch'd face.
BEATRICE	Scratching could not make it worse an 'twere such a face as yours were.
BENEDICK	Well, you are a rare parrot-teacher.
BEATRICE	A bird of my tongue is better than a beast of yours. 105
BENEDICK	I would my horse had the speed of your tongue, and so good a continuer. But keep your way, a God's name! I have done.
BEATRICE	You always end with a jade's trick. I know you of old.
DON PEDRO	That is the sum of all, Leonato. Signior Claudio and Signior 109 Benedick, my dear friend Leonato hath invited you all. I tell him we shall stay here at the least a month, and he heartily prays some occasion may detain us longer. I dare swear he is no hypocrite, but prays from his heart.
LEONATO	If you swear, my lord, you shall not be forsworn. [*To Don John*] Let me bid you welcome, my lord. Being reconciled to the Prince your brother, I owe you all duty. 116
DON JOHN	I thank you. I am not of many words, but I thank you.

---

90. **meet:** fit, appropriate. 91. **convert:** change. 93. **of:** by. 96. **dear:** great. The adjective *dear* is often used merely to emphasize the meaning of a noun. 97–98. **I am of your humor for that:** in *that* point my disposition agrees with yours. 100. **still:** always. 101. **predestinate:** inevitable [P.K.]. 104. **you are a rare parrot-teacher:** you talk no more sensibly than one who is teaching a parrot to speak words that mean nothing. 105. **A bird...yours:** A bird that speaks *my* language is better than a beast that has learned *yours*; for the language that you teach him is no language at all: he is a dumb beast. 106–7. **so good a continuer:** as tireless in his pace as your tongue is in talking. **—keep your way:** keep on; keep going. **—a God's name:** in God's name; for God's sake. 108. **with a jade's trick:** with some stupid remark that is as sensible as the tricks of a wretched nag. 109. **That is the sum of all:** That sums it all up. This is the concluding remark of a conversation that has been going on between Leonato and Don Pedro ("aside") while Benedick and Beatrice have been exchanging satirical jests.

LEONATO	Please it your Grace lead on?
DON PEDRO	Your hand, Leonato. We will go together.

Exeunt. Manent Benedick and Claudio.

CLAUDIO	Benedick, didst thou note the daughter of Signior Leonato?	120
BENEDICK	I noted her not, but I look'd on her.	
CLAUDIO	Is she not a modest young lady?	
BENEDICK	Do you question me, as an honest man should do, for my simple true judgment? or would you have me speak after my custom, as being a professed tyrant to their sex?	125
CLAUDIO	No. I pray thee speak in sober judgment.	
BENEDICK	Why, i' faith, methinks she's too low for a high praise, too brown for a fair praise, and too little for a great praise. Only this commendation I can afford her, that were she other than she is, she were unhandsome, and being no other but as she is, I do not like her.	131
CLAUDIO	Thou thinkest I am in sport. I pray thee tell me truly how thou lik'st her.	
BENEDICK	Would you buy her, that you enquire after her?	
CLAUDIO	Can the world buy such a jewel?	135
BENEDICK	Yea, and a case to put it into. But speak you this with a sad brow? or do you play the flouting Jack, to tell us Cupid is a good hare-finder and Vulcan a rare carpenter? Come, in what key shall a man take you to go in the song?	
CLAUDIO	In mine eye she is the sweetest lady that ever I look'd on.	140
BENEDICK	I can see yet without spectacles, and I see no such matter. There's her cousin, an she were not possess'd with a fury, exceeds her as much in beauty as the first of May doth the last of December. But I hope you have no intent to turn husband, have you?	144
CLAUDIO	I would scarce trust myself, though I had sworn the contrary, if Hero would be my wife.	

Stage direction. **Manent:** stay behind. 119. **We will go together.** Thus Don Pedro refuses to take precedence of Leonato. 121. **I noted her not:** Benedick perceives that Claudio has been attracted by Hero (who has spoken only once in this scene), and he proceeds to have some fun with him. 123–4. **simple true:** plain-spoken and sincere. 136–8. **speak you this...carpenter?** When you call her "a jewel," are you speaking in earnest, or are you joking around, as if you were to call blind Cupid a keen-eyed hunter or to call Vulcan, the god of fire and the armorer of the gods, a first-rate carpenter? —**sad:** serious. —**flouting Jack:** mocking fellow. 139. **to go in the song?** in order to be in harmony with your mood.141. **no such matter:** nothing of the kind. 142. **possess'd with a fury:** as sharp-tongued as if one of the Furies had taken possession of her. The Furies, in Greek mythology, were the goddesses of vengeance and retaliation. [P.K.]

BENEDICK	Is't come to this? In faith, hath not the world one man but he will wear his cap with suspicion? Shall I never see a bachelor of threescore again? Go to, i' faith! An thou wilt needs thrust thy neck into a yoke, wear the print of it and sigh away Sundays. 150

Enter Don Pedro.

	Look! Don Pedro is returned to seek you.
DON PEDRO	What secret hath held you here, that you followed not to Leonato's?
BENEDICK	I would your Grace would constrain me to tell.
DON PEDRO	I charge thee on thy allegiance. 155
BENEDICK	You hear, Count Claudio. I can be secret as a dumb man, I would have you think so; but, on my allegiance—mark you this—on my allegiance! he is in love. With who? Now that is your Grace's part. Mark how short his answer is: With Hero, Leonato's short daughter. 160
CLAUDIO	If this were so, so were it utt'red.
BENEDICK	Like the old tale, my lord: "It is not so, nor 'twas not so; but indeed, God forbid it should be so!"
CLAUDIO	If my passion change not shortly, God forbid it should be otherwise. 165
DON PEDRO	Amen, if you love her; for the lady is very well worthy.
CLAUDIO	You speak this to fetch me in, my lord.
DON PEDRO	By my troth, I speak my thought.
CLAUDIO	And, in faith, my lord, I spoke mine.
BENEDICK	And, by my two faiths and troths, my lord, I spoke mine. 170

147–8. **but...suspicion:** who will not run the risk of getting married and thus being forced always to suspect that his wife has been false to him. A husband, he insinuates, never knows whether horns have not grown on his head (the sign of being a cuckold) since he put on his cap. 149. **Go to!** An interjection of protest, like our "Come on!" —**sigh away Sundays:** spend your Sundays (which should be days of rest and refreshment) in sorrow; spend all your leisure time in sadness. 158–9. **that is your Grace's part:** it is your Grace's part to ask that question. 161. **If this were so, so were it utt'red:** If I were really in love with Hero and had confided in Benedick, this is precisely the satirical fashion in which he would reveal my secret. Claudio is not quite ready to admit that he is in love, but he confesses it in his next speech. 162. **Like the old tale, etc.** The tale is a version of the Bluebeard story. The heroine, who has visited the murderer's house, is relating her gruesome discoveries, pretending it was all a dream. The murderer, who is present, cries out, as she mentions one horror after another: "It is not so, nor it was not so, and God forbid it should be so!" 164–5. **God forbid...otherwise:** God forbid that I should not be in love with her. 167. **to fetch me in:** to take me in; to trick me into making admissions, giving myself away. 170. **by my two faiths and troths:** *two*—since I am speaking to both of you.

CLAUDIO	That I love her, I feel.
DON PEDRO	That she is worthy, I know.
BENEDICK	That I neither feel how she should be loved, nor know how she should be worthy, is the opinion that fire cannot melt out of me. I will die in it at the stake. 175
DON PEDRO	Thou wast ever an obstinate heretic in the despite of beauty.
CLAUDIO	And never could maintain his part but in the force of his will.
BENEDICK	That a woman conceived me, I thank her; that she brought me up, I likewise give her most humble thanks; but that I will have a rechate winded in my forehead, or hang my bugle in an invisible baldrick, all women shall pardon me. Because I will not do them the wrong to mistrust any, I will do myself the right to trust none; and the fine is (for the which I may go the finer), I will live a bachelor.
DON PEDRO	I shall see thee, ere I die, look pale with love. 185
BENEDICK	With anger, with sickness, or with hunger, my lord; not with love. Prove that ever I lose more blood with love than I will get again with drinking, pick out mine eyes with a ballad-maker's pen and hang me up at the door of a brothel house for the sign of blind Cupid. 190
DON PEDRO	Well, if ever thou dost fall from this faith, thou wilt prove a notable argument.
BENEDICK	If I do, hang me in a bottle like a cat and shoot at me; and he that hits me, let him be clapp'd on the shoulder and call'd Adam.
DON PEDRO	Well, as time shall try. 195 "In time the savage bull doth bear the yoke."

---

176. **in the despite of:** in showing scorn for. 177. **never...will:** and never could show any moderation in arguing for his heretical opinions, but always supported them stubbornly. 178–84. **That a woman... bachelor.** Benedick speaks with mock solemnity, as if he were reciting his heretical confession of faith. —**but that I will...pardon me:** but all women must excuse me from consenting to wear a horn on which every huntsman can blow; i.e., from being a confessed and notorious cuckold. —**rechate:** a signal on a huntsman's horn to call back the dogs. —**hang...baldrick:** carry a bugle horn in an invisible belt; i.e., be a cuckold without knowing it. —**the fine:** the conclusion of the whole matter. —**may go the finer:** may dress in finer apparel (since I shall not have to support a wife). 187. **lose more blood with love:** Sighing and sorrow were thought to exhaust the blood. Every sigh was said to draw a drop of blood from the heart. 188. **with a ballad-maker's pen:** with the pen of a writer of sorrowful love-songs. 191. **this faith:** this heretical doctrine that you have just set forth so elaborately. 192. **a notable argument:** a noteworthy subject of conversation; an instance that will often be cited as remarkable. 193. **in a bottle like a cat:** To shoot at a cat hung up in a basket or a wooden jar was a rustic diversion. 194. **Adam:** Adam Bell, a famous archer in an old ballad. 195. **Well, as time shall try:** Well, we'll leave your fate to time.

BENEDICK	The savage bull may; but if ever the sensible Benedick bear it, pluck off the bull's horns and set them in my forehead, and let me be vilely painted, and in such great letters as they write "Here is good horse to hire," let them signify under my sign "Here you may see Benedick the married man." 201
CLAUDIO	If this should ever happen, thou wouldst be horn-mad.
DON PEDRO	Nay, if Cupid have not spent all his quiver in Venice, thou wilt quake for this shortly.
BENEDICK	I look for an earthquake too then. 205
DON PEDRO	Well, you will temporize with the hours. In the meantime, good Signior Benedick, repair to Leonato's, commend me to him and tell him I will not fail him at supper; for indeed he hath made great preparation. 209
BENEDICK	I have almost matter enough in me for such an embassage; and so I commit you—
CLAUDIO	To the tuition of God. From my house—if I had it—
DON PEDRO	The sixth of July. Your loving friend, Benedick.
BENEDICK	Nay, mock not, mock not. The body of your discourse is sometime guarded with fragments, and the guards are but slightly basted on neither. Ere you flout old ends any further, examine your conscience. And so I leave you. [*Exit*] 217
CLAUDIO	My liege, your Highness now may do me good.
DON PEDRO	My love is thine to teach. Teach it but how, And thou shalt see how apt it is to learn 220 Any hard lesson that may do thee good.
CLAUDIO	Hath Leonato any son, my lord?
DON PEDRO	No child but Hero; she's his only heir. Dost thou affect her, Claudio?

198–9. let me be vilely painted, etc.: have a wretched picture of me (with horns in my forehead) painted, and set it up on a pole in front of the showman's booth where I am on exhibition as a monster; and under this sign give notice to the public, in large letters, "Here —," etc. **202. horn-mad.** An old expression for "stark mad," "raving mad." Its origin is uncertain, but it was often brought into punning connection (as here) with the horns of a cuckold. **203. spent all his quiver:** emptied his quiver; used up all his arrows. **—in Venice.** In Shakespeare's time Venice was famous for its courtesans. **206. you will temporize with the hours:** you will adapt yourself to the hours; as time goes on, you will have to adapt your sentiments and conduct to the changes that time brings with it. **207. commend me to him:** give him my regards. **210. matter:** mental material; intellect. **212. To the tuition, etc.:** In imitation of the formal close of a letter. **—tuition:** protection, guardianship. **213. The sixth of July:** Old Midsummer Day, an appropriate date for such midsummer madness. **215. guarded:** trimmed. **216. flout:** make fun of, mock. **—old ends:** old scraps (odds and ends) of proverbial wisdom. **220. apt:** ready. **224. Dost thou affect her?** Are you attracted to her?

CLAUDIO   O my lord,
                When you went onward on this ended action,   225
                I look'd upon her with a soldier's eye,
                That lik'd, but had a rougher task in hand
                Than to drive liking to the name of love;
                But now I am return'd and that war-thoughts
                Have left their places vacant, in their rooms   230
                Come thronging soft and delicate desires,
                All prompting me how fair young Hero is,
                Saying I lik'd her ere I went to wars.

DON PEDRO   Thou wilt be like a lover presently
                And tire the hearer with a book of words.   235
                If thou dost love fair Hero, cherish it,
                And I will break with her and with her father,
                And thou shalt have her. Was't not to this end
                That thou began'st to twist so fine a story?

CLAUDIO   How sweetly you do minister to love,   240
                That know love's grief by his complexion!
                But lest my liking might too sudden seem,
                I would have salv'd it with a longer treatise.

DON PEDRO   What need the bridge much broader than the flood?
                The fairest grant is the necessity.   245
                Look, what will serve is fit. 'Tis once, thou lovest,
                And I will fit thee with the remedy.
                I know we shall have reveling tonight.
                I will assume thy part in some disguise
                And tell fair Hero I am Claudio,   250
                And in her bosom I'll unclasp my heart
                And take her hearing prisoner with the force
                And strong encounter of my amorous tale.
                Then after to her father will I break,
                And the conclusion is, she shall be thine.   255
                In practice let us put it presently.   *Exeunt.*

---

225. **this ended action:** this war that is just finished. 236. **cherish it:** cherish that love. 237. **break with her:** broach the matter to her. 239. **to twist:** to knit up, compose. Don Pedro smiles at the elaboration of Claudio's speech. 240. **minister to:** help; do service to. Claudio is thanking Don Pedro for his offer to speak to Hero and her father in his behalf. 241. **his:** its. 242–3. **lest...treatise:** for fear you might think my love too sudden, I was disposed to use even more words in order to make it seem less abrupt in the telling. Claudio is explaining why he has "twisted so fine a story." 245. **The fairest grant is the necessity:** The best favor one can receive is to have what one needs. 246. **what will serve is fit:** Anything that will answer the purpose is suitable. —**'Tis once:** There's just one thing to bear in mind. 248. **reveling:** festivity. 251. **in...heart:** to her in private I'll disclose my love (i.e., your love, for I shall be playing your part). 256. **presently:** without delay or loss of time.

SCENE II. [*A room in Leonato's house.*]

*Enter [at one door] Leonato and [at another door, Antonio,]
an old man, brother to Leonato.*

LEONATO   How now, brother? Where is my cousin your son? Hath he
provided this music?

ANTONIO   He is very busy about it. But, brother, I can tell you strange news
that you yet dreamt not of.

LEONATO   Are they good?   5

ANTONIO   As the event stamps them; but they have a good cover, they show
well outward. The Prince and Count Claudio, walking in a thick-
pleached alley in mine orchard, were thus much overheard by a
man of mine: the Prince discovered to Claudio that he loved my
niece your daughter and meant to acknowledge it this night in   10
a dance, and if he found her accordant, he meant to take the
present time by the top and instantly break with you of it.

LEONATO   Hath the fellow any wit that told you this?

ANTONIO   A good sharp fellow. I will send for him, and question him
yourself.   15

LEONATO   No, no. We will hold it as a dream till it appear itself; but I will
acquaint my daughter withal, that she may be the better prepared
for an answer, if peradventure this be true. Go you and tell her
of it.   [*Exit Antonio.*]

[Enter Antonio's Son with a Musician, and others.]

[*To the Son*] Cousin, you know what you have to do.—[*To the*   20
Musician] O, I cry you mercy, friend. Go you with me, and I will
use your skill.—Good cousin, have a care this busy time.

Exeunt.

SCENE II.
1. **cousin:** nephew. *Cousin* was a general word, not merely for "cousin" in our sense, but for "nephew"
or "niece," "uncle" or "aunt." This nephew of Leonato's appears in the present scene only and is never
mentioned afterwards. 5. **they:** *News* was originally plural—"new things." 6. **the event:** the outcome,
the result. —**they have a good cover:** The next sentence explains this. —**show:** appear. 7–8. **thick-
pleached:** closely screened by vines and hedges. To *pleach* is to "plait." —**in mine orchard.** Leonato
and his brother Antonio live together in the same mansion—a vast establishment with elaborately
laid-out grounds. *Orchard* means "garden"—not, as in modern usage, a mere plantation of fruit trees.
9. **discovered:** disclosed, revealed. The servant had overheard only a part of the conversation between
Claudio and Don Pedro; and he had misunderstood what he heard, supposing that Don Pedro meant to
woo Hero for himself. He did not know that Don Pedro was to impersonate Claudio in the masquerade.
11. **accordant:** in accord with his wishes. 11–12. **to take the present time by the top:** to take time
by the forelock. —**break with you of it:** open the subject to you. —**of it:** concerning it. 13. **any wit:**
any sense. 16. **till it appear itself:** until it present itself as a fact. 17. **withal:** with it. 18. **peradventure:**
perhaps. 21. **I cry you mercy:** I beg your pardon. 22. **have a care:** keep an eye on things.

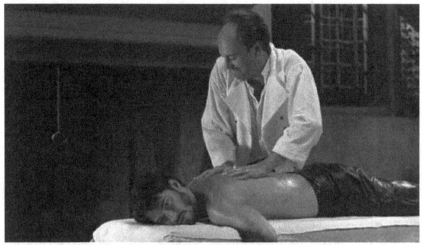

Conrade and Don John conspire in Kenneth Branagh's *Much Ado About Nothing*. (1993)

SCENE III. [*Another room in Leonato's house.*]

Enter Sir John the Bastard and Conrade, his companion.

CONRADE   What the goodyear, my lord! Why are you thus out of measure
             sad?†

DON JOHN   There is no measure in the occasion that breeds; therefore the
             sadness is without limit.

CONRADE   You should hear reason.   5

DON JOHN   And when I have heard it, what blessing brings it?

CONRADE   If not a present remedy, at least a patient sufferance.

DON JOHN   I wonder that thou (being, as thou say'st thou art, born under
             Saturn) goest about to apply a moral medicine to a mortifying
             mischief. I cannot hide what I am: I must be sad when I have
             cause, and smile at no man's jests; eat when I have stomach, and

---

SCENE III.
1. **What the goodyear!** What the mischief is the matter? An old slang phrase of unknown origin. 3. **that breeds:** that causes my sadness. 8–9. **born under Saturn:** born when Saturn was the ruling planet, and therefore of a Saturnian (or Saturnine) disposition—prone to every kind of dismal wickedness. 9–10. **goest about...mischief:** try to cure the deadly melancholy of my disposition by mere moralizing. *Mischief* is common in the sense of "disease." 11. **stomach:** appetite.

---

†   In Branagh's film, Conrade is massaging a shirtless Don John lying on a table in a steamy room during the early part of this scene. Antoon has Don John shooting a pistol (unsuccessfully) at a duck in a pond from the gazebo at night while he discusses his melancholy with Conrade. Where Branagh's Don John is menacing, Antoon's is comically malicious. [P.K.]

wait for no man's leisure; sleep when I am drowsy, and tend on no man's business; laugh when I am merry, and claw no man in his humor.   14

CONRADE   Yea, but you must not make the full show of this till you may do it without controlment. You have of late stood out against your brother, and he hath ta'en you newly into his grace where it is impossible you should take true root but by the fair weather that you make yourself. It is needful that you frame the season for your own harvest.   20

DON JOHN   I had rather be a canker in a hedge than a rose in his grace, and it better fits my blood to be disdain'd of all than to fashion a carriage to rob love from any. In this, though I cannot be said to be a flattering honest man, it must not be denied but I am a plain-dealing villain. I am trusted with a muzzle and enfranchis'd with a clog; therefore I have decreed not to sing in my cage. If I had my mouth, I would bite; if I had my liberty, I would do my liking. In the meantime let me be that I am, and seek not to alter me.

CONRADE   Can you make no use of your discontent?

DON JOHN   I make all use of it, for I use it only.   30

Enter Borachio.

Who comes here? What news, Borachio?

BORACHIO   I came yonder from a great supper. The Prince your brother is royally entertain'd by Leonato, and I can give you intelligence of an intended marriage.

DON JOHN   Will it serve for any model to build mischief on? What is he for   35
a fool that betroths himself to unquietness?

BORACHIO   Marry, it is your brother's right hand.

DON JOHN   Who? the most exquisite Claudio?

BORACHIO   Even he.

13–14. **claw...humor:** adapt myself to no man's likes and dislikes. To *claw* means, literally, to "scratch," and hence it came to signify to "please" or "flatter"—as scratching is a relief when one itches. 16. **without controlment:** without being called to account for it. To *control* often means to "rebuke" or "restrain." —**stood out:** rebelled. 17. **grace:** favor. Thus we learn that Don John has been forgiven by his brother and that he feels the resentment which too often is cherished by a pardoned offender. 21. **I had rather be a canker...grace:** I had rather be an independent outcast than a prince's favorite courtier. A *canker* (also called *dog rose*) is a wild rose. 22. **blood:** disposition, temper. —**of all:** by everybody. 22–23. **to fashion...any:** to assume such a manner as shall by its hypocrisy win the undeserved affection of anybody. 26. **decreed:** decided, determined. 28. **that I am:** what I am in fact. 29. **use:** profitable employment. 30. **I use it only:** I practice it exclusively. Don John puns bitterly on Conrade's word *use*. 33. **intelligence:** information. 35. **model:** ground plan. 35–36. **What is he for a fool?** What kind of fool is he? 37. **Marry:** why. *Marry* was originally an oath by the Virgin Mary, but it came to be used as a mere interjection.

DON JOHN	A proper squire! And who? and who? which way looks he? 40
BORACHIO	Marry, on Hero, the daughter and heir of Leonato.
DON JOHN	A very forward March-chick! How came you to this?
BORACHIO	Being entertain'd for a perfumer, as I was smoking a musty room, comes me the Prince and Claudio, hand in hand in sad conference. I whipt me behind the arras and there heard it agreed upon that the Prince should woo Hero for himself, and having obtain'd her, give her to Count Claudio.
DON JOHN	Come, come, let us thither. This may prove food to my displeasure. That young start-up hath all the glory of my overthrow. If I can cross him any way, I bless myself every way. You are both sure, 50 and will assist me?
CONRADE	To the death, my lord.
DON JOHN	Let us to the great supper. Their cheer is the greater that I am subdued. Would the cook were o' my mind! Shall we go prove what's to be done? 55
BORACHIO	We'll wait upon your lordship. *Exeunt.*

ACT II

SCENE I. [*A hall in Leonato's house.*]

Enter Leonato, [Antonio] his Brother, Hero his Daughter,
and Beatrice his Niece, and a Kinsman; [also Margaret and Ursula].†

| LEONATO | Was not Count John here at supper? |
| ANTONIO | I saw him not. |

---

40. **proper:** handsome. 42. **forward March-chick:** precocious young one. 43. **entertain'd:** engaged; hired. —**smoking:** fumigating (by burning aromatic substances). 44. **sad:** serious. 45. **the arras:** the tapestry hangings. The conversation overheard (and misunderstood) by Borachio must have taken place in the interval between 1.1 and 1.2 after Don Pedro and Claudio had left the garden and entered Leonato's house. 48. **my displeasure:** my misanthropy. 49. **start-up:** upstart. —**my overthrow:** i.e., in my rebellion against Don Pedro 50. **cross:** thwart. —**sure:** trustworthy; to be depended on. 53. **cheer:** festivity—especially in the way of good things to eat. 54–55. **prove what's to be done:** try to find out what we can do in the way of thwarting Claudio's plans. 56. **wait upon:** accompany you as attendants.

---

† Before the men arrive on scene in Antoon's film, the women, prompted by Beatrice, are secretly sharing a cigarette, a very "un-ladylike" thing to do in early twentieth-century small-town America. [P.K.]

BEATRICE	How tartly that gentleman looks! I never can see him but I am heart-burn'd an hour after.	
HERO	He is of a very melancholy disposition.	5
BEATRICE	He were an excellent man that were made just in the midway between him and Benedick. The one is too like an image and says nothing, and the other too like my lady's eldest son, evermore tattling.	9
LEONATO	Then half Signior Benedick's tongue in Count John's mouth, and half Count John's melancholy in Signior Benedick's face—	
BEATRICE	With a good leg and a good foot, uncle, and money enough in his purse, such a man would win any woman in the world—if 'a could get her good will.	14
LEONATO	By my troth, niece, thou wilt never get thee a husband if thou be so shrewd of thy tongue.	
ANTONIO	In faith, she's too curst.	
BEATRICE	Too curst is more than curst. I shall lessen God's sending that way, for it is said, "God sends a curst cow short horns," but to a cow too curst he sends none.	20
LEONATO	So, by being too curst, God will send you no horns.	
BEATRICE	Just, if he send me no husband; for the which blessing I am at him upon my knees every morning and evening. Lord, I could not endure a husband with a beard on his face. I had rather lie in the woolen!	25
LEONATO	You may light on a husband that hath no beard.	
BEATRICE	What should I do with him? dress him in my apparel and make him my waiting gentlewoman? He that hath a beard is more than a youth, and he that hath no beard is less than a man; and he that is more than a youth is not for me; and he that is less than a man, I am not for him. Therefore I will even take sixpence in earnest of the berrord and lead his apes into hell.	32
LEONATO	Well then, go you into hell?	

ACT II. SCENE I.
3. **tartly:** sour. 8. **my lady's eldest son:** a spoiled child. 16. **shrewd of thy tongue:** shrewish, satirical. *Curst* is synonymous. 18. **that way:** in that regard. 19. **God sends...short horns.** An old proverb, often used to illustrate God's providential care of men. *Curst* means ill-tempered. 22. **Just:** just so; quite right. 24–25. **in the woolen:** in rough woolen blankets without sheets. 31. **in earnest of the berrord:** as a payment in advance to bind the bargain by which I become the bear-keeper's assistant. 32. **lead his apes into hell.** The proverb was very common in use. It implies that such was the punishment for a woman who had refused to do her duty in this world—namely, to marry and bear children. —**his apes.** A bear-keeper often had a number of performing apes in his charge.

BEATRICE	No; but to the gate, and there will the devil meet me like an old cuckold with horns on his head, and say "Get you to heaven, 35 Beatrice, get you to heaven. Here's no place for you maids." So deliver I up my apes, and away to Saint Peter—for the heavens. He shows me where the bachelors sit, and there live we as merry as the day is long.
ANTONIO	[*to Hero*] Well, niece, I trust you will be rul'd by your father. 40
BEATRICE	Yes faith. It is my cousin's duty to make curtsy and say, "Father, as it please you." But yet for all that, cousin, let him be a handsome fellow, or else make another curtsy, and say, "Father, as it please me."
LEONATO	Well, niece, I hope to see you one day fitted with a husband. 45
BEATRICE	Not till God make men of some other metal than earth. Would it not grieve a woman to be overmaster'd with a piece of valiant dust? to make an account of her life to a clod of wayward marl? No, uncle, I'll none. Adam's sons are my brethren, and truly I hold it a sin to match in my kindred. 50
LEONATO	Daughter, remember what I told you. If the Prince do solicit you in that kind, you know your answer.
BEATRICE	The fault will be in the music, cousin, if you be not wooed in good time. If the Prince be too important, tell him there is measure in everything, and so dance out the answer. For, hear me, Hero: wooing, wedding, and repenting is as a Scotch jig, a measure, and a cinquepace: the first suit is hot and hasty like a Scotch jig—and full as fantastical; the wedding, mannerly modest, as a measure, full of state and ancientry; and then comes Repentance and with his bad legs falls into the cinquepace faster and faster, till he sink into his grave. 61
LEONATO	Cousin, you apprehend passing shrewdly.

---

34. **like:** in the guise of. 37. **for the heavens:** bound for heaven; on my heavenward journey. 38–39. **as merry...long.** Beatrice remembers the text: "For when they shall rise from the dead, they neither marry nor are given in marriage; but are as the angels which are in heaven" (Mark 12:25). 40. **Well, niece, I trust you will be rul'd by your father.** Antonio and Leonato mistakenly suppose that Don Pedro means to woo Hero for himself, and it is clear from the present scene that Leonato has already told her that she is to accept him. Hero makes no reply to her uncle's remark. Perhaps her silence gives consent. Probably, however, it is an indication of reluctance; for doubtless she has already fallen in love with Claudio (as he with her) at first sight. At all events, she soon learns from Don Pedro (who impersonates Claudio in the masquerade) that he is wooing her for Claudio. 46 **metal:** material. 47. **with:** by. 48. **gloss:** clay. 49. **I'll none:** I'll have no husband. 52. **in that kind:** in that regard; i.e., with reference to marriage. 53–54. **in good time:** with due regard to decorum; with such humility as befits a suitor. —**too important:** too demanding—antithetic to "in good time." —**a measure:** a stately dance, like a minuet. 57. **a cinque-pace:** a rapid and lively kind of dance. 59. **state and ancientry:** antique stateliness. 62. **you apprehend passing shrewdly:** Your apprehensions (your ideas about things) are extremely keen and bitter. —**passing.** An adverb—"surpassingly."

BEATRICE   I have a good eye, uncle; I can see a church by daylight.

LEONATO   The revellers are ent'ring, brother. Make good room.[*Exit Antonio.*]

Enter, [masked,] Don Pedro, Claudio, Benedick, and Balthasar.
[With them enter Antonio, also masked. After them enter] Don John
[and Borachio (without masks), who stand aside and look on during the dance]†.

DON PEDRO   Lady, will you walk a bout with your friend?   65

HERO   So you walk softly and look sweetly and say nothing, I am yours for the walk; and especially when I walk away.

DON PEDRO   With me in your company?

HERO   I may say so when I please.

DON PEDRO   And when please you to say so?   70

HERO   When I like your favor, for God defend the lute should be like the case!

DON PEDRO   My visor is Philemon's roof; within the house is Jove.

HERO   Why then, your visor should be thatch'd.

DON PEDRO   Speak low if you speak love.   [*Takes her aside.*] 75

BALTHASAR   Well, I would you did like me.

MARGARET   So would not I for your own sake, for I have many ill qualities.

BALTHASAR   Which is one?

MARGARET   I say my prayers aloud.

BALTHASAR   I love you the better. The hearers may cry Amen.   80

MARGARET   God match me with a good dancer!

BALTHASAR   Amen.

---

64. **Make good room:** See that the hall is made clear for the maskers. 65. **a bout:** a turn in the dance. —**friend:** Intentionally ambiguous; *friend* often meant "lover." 66. **So:** provided that. 71. **favor:** features, looks. —**defend:** forbid. 73. **visor:** mask. —**Jove:** Thus Pedro suggests his identity. In Roman mythology, Jove (also called Jupiter) was the ruler of the gods [P.K.]. 74. **should be thatch'd:** should have thatch instead of hair, because the house of Baucis and Philemon, the humble entertainers of the disguised Jupiter (Jove), was thatched with straw. 77. **qualities:** traits of character.

---

† Antoon, Burge and Branagh all stage this scene as an elaborate set piece, with festive music and expressive carnival masks. In Antoon's film, the masquers waltz to the music of a brass band. In Branagh, they dance outdoors by candlelight. Burge locates them in great hall of the palazzo. The *Shakespeare Retold* adaptation sets the scene at a costume party, in which the choice of apparel comments on the characters: Benedick and Claude (Claudio) appear as knights, Beatrice as Queen Elizabeth I, Hero as Marilyn Monroe, Leonard (Leonato) as a Roman emperor, and Don (Don John) as the Joker.

Benedick and Beatrice at the ball in Antoon's *Much Ado*. (1973)

MARGARET	And God keep him out of my sight when the dance is done! Answer, clerk.
BALTHASAR	No more words. The clerk is answered. [*Takes her aside.*] 85
URSULA	I know you well enough. You are Signior Antonio.
ANTONIO	At a word, I am not.
URSULA	I know you by the waggling of your head.
ANTONIO	To tell you true, I counterfeit him. 89
URSULA	You could never do him so ill-well unless you were the very man. Here's his dry hand up and down. You are he, you are he!
ANTONIO	At a word, I am not.
URSULA	Come, come, do you think I do not know you by your excellent wit? Can virtue hide itself? Go to, mum, you are he. Graces will appear, and there's an end. [*They step aside.*] 95
BEATRICE	Will you not tell me who told you so?

84. **Answer, clerk.** It was the parish clerk's office to make the responses in the church service. Balthasar, Margaret implies, has been playing a clerk's part in saying "Amen." 85. **The clerk is answered:** If I am the clerk, I am answered instead of answering. Therefore I have nothing more to say. 87. **At a word:** to answer you briefly and positively. 90. **do him so ill-well:** imitate him so well in his feebleness. 91. **his dry hand:** A traditional symptom of old age or debility. —**up and down:** out and out; exactly. 94. **virtue:** excellence of any kind. —**Graces:** good qualities. 95. **there's an end:** that's all there is to it; there's no more to be said.

BENEDICK	No, you shall pardon me.
BEATRICE	Nor will you not tell me who you are?
BENEDICK	Not now.
BEATRICE	That I was disdainful, and that I had my good wit out of the 100 "Hundred Merry Tales." Well, this was Signior Benedick that said so.
BENEDICK	What's he?
BEATRICE	I am sure you know him well enough.
BENEDICK	Not I, believe me. 105
BEATRICE	Did he never make you laugh?
BENEDICK	I pray you, what is he?
BEATRICE	Why, he is the Prince's jester, a very dull fool. Only his gift is in devising impossible slanders. None but libertines delight in him; and the commendation is not in his wit, but in his villainy; for he both pleases men and angers them, and then they laugh at him and beat him. I am sure he is in the fleet. I would he had boarded me.
BENEDICK	When I know the gentleman, I'll tell him what you say.
BEATRICE	Do, do. He'll but break a comparison or two on me; which 115 peradventure, not marked or not laugh'd at, strikes him into melancholy; and then there's a partridge wing saved, for the fool will eat no supper that night. [*Music.*] We must follow the leaders.
BENEDICK	In every good thing. 120
BEATRICE	Nay, if they lead to any ill, I will leave them at the next turning.

Dance. Exeunt [all but Don John, Borachio, and Claudio].

DON JOHN	Sure my brother is amorous on Hero and hath withdrawn her father to break with him about it. The ladies follow her and but one visor remains.

---

97. **you shall pardon me:** you must excuse me from telling. 101. **the "Hundred Merry Tales."** A coarsely humorous book, very popular in Shakespeare's day. 109. **libertines:** people with loose morals [P.K.]. 110. **the commendation:** that which recommends him to them; that for which they like him. —**villainy:** his malicious satire. 112. **in the fleet:** somewhere in this company of maskers. —**boarded;** To *board* often meant simply to "accost," to "speak to." Hence the pun. 116. **peradventure:** perhaps. 119. **follow the leaders:** i.e., in the dance. 121. **turning:** Beatrice puns, as usual. *Turning* means (1) "a turning in the road," "a by-road," and (2) "a movement in the dance." 122. **Sure my brother is amorous on Hero:** Don John had supposed that his brother meant to woo Hero for Claudio, but Don Pedro has been acting the part of a lover so well that Don John is persuaded that he had actually fallen in love with her. We are not to suppose that Claudio heard this remark.

BORACHIO	And that is Claudio. I know him by his bearing.	125
DON JOHN	Are you not Signior Benedick?	
CLAUDIO	You know me well. I am he.	
DON JOHN	Signior, you are very near my brother in his love. He is enamour'd on Hero. I pray you dissuade him from her; she is no equal for his birth. You may do the part of an honest man in it.	130
CLAUDIO	How know you he loves her?	
DON JOHN	I heard him swear his affection.	
BORACHIO	So did I too, and he swore he would marry her tonight.	
DON JOHN	Come, let us to the banquet. *Exeunt. Manet Claudio.*	
CLAUDIO	Thus answer I in name of Benedick,	135
	But hear these ill news with the ears of Claudio.	
	'Tis certain so. The Prince woos for himself.	
	Friendship is constant in all other things	
	Save in the office and affairs of love.	
	Therefore all hearts in love use their own tongues;	140
	Let every eye negotiate for itself	
	And trust no agent; for beauty is a witch	
	Against whose charms faith melteth into blood.	
	This is an accident of hourly proof,	
	Which I mistrusted not. Farewell therefore Hero!	145
	Enter Benedick.	
BENEDICK	Count Claudio?	
CLAUDIO	Yea, the same.	
BENEDICK	Come, will you go with me?	
CLAUDIO	Whither?	149
BENEDICK	Even to the next willow, about your own business, County. What fashion will you wear the garland of? about your neck, like an usurer's chain? or under your arm, like a lieutenant's scarf? You	

---

128. **very near...love:** a very intimate friend of my brother's. 130. **honest:** honorable. 133. **tonight:** This modifies *swore*. Marriages were celebrated in the morning. 134. **banquet:** a light meal of wine and sweets. 136. **these ill news:** *News* is plural. 139. **the office:** the business. 140. **all hearts use:** let all hearts use. 143. **Against whose charms:** when exposed to whose spells. —**melteth:** The allusion is to image magic, which has been prevalent from very ancient times. An effigy of wax, clay, wood, metal, or almost any substance, is pierced with nails, pins, or thorns, and burned or slowly roasted. The victim is expected to suffer corresponding torments, to pine away as the puppet melts or crumbles, and to die when it is stabbed to the heart. —**blood:** passion. 144. **accident of hourly proof:** an occurrence of which every hour affords an example. 150. **willow:** The weeping willow was a symbol for grief and especially for the grief of disconsolate lovers. A willow garland was the wreath that such a lover was said to wear. —**County:** Count. 152. **an usurer's chain:** A long gold chain was a regular adornment in a rich man's attire.

	must wear it one way, for the Prince hath got your Hero.	
CLAUDIO	I wish him joy of her.	154
BENEDICK	Why, that's spoken like an honest drovier. So they sell bullocks. But did you think the Prince would have served you thus?	
CLAUDIO	I pray you leave me.	
BENEDICK	Ho! now you strike like the blind man! 'Twas the boy that stole your meat, and you'll beat the post.	
CLAUDIO	If it will not be, I'll leave you. *Exit.* 160	
BENEDICK	Alas, poor hurt fowl! now will he creep into sedges. But, that my Lady Beatrice should know me, and not know me! The Prince's fool! Ha! it may be I go under that title because I am merry. Yea, but so I am apt to do myself wrong. I am not so reputed. It is the base (though bitter) disposition of Beatrice that puts the world into 165 her person and so gives me out. Well, I'll be revenged as I may.	

Enter Don Pedro

DON PEDRO	Now, signior, where's the Count? Did you see him?	167
BENEDICK	Troth, my lord, I have played the part of Lady Fame. I found him here as melancholy as a lodge in a warren. I told him, and I think I told him true, that your Grace had got the good will of this young lady, and I off'red him my company to a willow tree, either to make him a garland, as being forsaken, or to bind him up a rod, as being worthy to be whipt.	
DON PEDRO	To be whipt? What's his fault?	174
BENEDICK	The flat transgression of a schoolboy who, being overjoyed with finding a bird's nest, shows it his companion, and he steals it.	
DON PEDRO	Wilt thou make a trust a transgression? The transgression is in the stealer.	

---

155. **drovier:** drover, cattle-dealer. —**So they sell bullocks:** Benedick means that, when the drover sells an animal, he wishes the purchaser good luck. 159. **the post:** Benedick puns on *post* in the sense of "messenger"—the person who brought you the news but who is not guilty of the offence for which you are angry. He alludes to some comic tale in which a blind man lashes a post, thinking he is punishing a thievish boy. The tale has not been identified. 160. **If...you:** If it is impossible to induce *you* to leave *me, I'll* leave *you.* 164. **so...reputed:** in *that* conclusion (in thinking I am known as the Prince's fool) I am too ready to do myself an injustice, for I am sure I have no such reputation. 164–66. **It is the base (though bitter)...gives me out:** It is Beatrice's contemptible disposition that (ascribing to the whole world her own personal feelings with regard to me) thus describes me; but, though I may regard her disposition as contemptible, I find that I am stung by it—I cannot bear her slander without cringing. 166. **as I may:** as best I can. 168. **Troth:** by my faith. —**Lady Fame:** The goddess of report and rumor. 169. **in a warren:** i.e., in a rabbit warren—a solitary and melancholy place. 175. **The flat transgression of a schoolboy:** nothing more or less than the error of a stupid schoolboy.

BENEDICK	Yet it had not been amiss the rod had been made, and the garland too; for the garland he might have worn himself, and the rod he might have bestowed on you, who, as I take it, have stol'n his bird's nest. 182
DON PEDRO	I will but teach them to sing and restore them to the owner.
BENEDICK	If their singing answer your saying, by my faith you say honestly.
DON PEDRO	The Lady Beatrice hath a quarrel to you. The gentleman that 185 danc'd with her told her she is much wrong'd by you.
BENEDICK	O, she misus'd me past the endurance of a block! An oak but with one green leaf on it would have answered her; my very visor began to assume life and scold with her. She told me, not thinking I had been myself, that I was the Prince's jester, that I was duller than a great thaw; huddling jest upon jest with such impossible conveyance upon me that I stood like a man at a mark, with a whole army shooting at me. She speaks poniards, and every word stabs. If her breath were as terrible as her terminations, there were no living near her; she would infect to the North Star. I would not marry her though she were endowed with all that Adam had left him before he transgress'd. She would have made Hercules have turn'd spit, yea, and have cleft his club to make the fire too. Come, talk not of her. You shall find her the infernal Ate in good apparel. I would to God some scholar would conjure her, for certainly, while she is here, a man may live as quiet in hell as in a sanctuary; and people sin upon purpose, because they would go thither; so indeed all disquiet, horror, and perturbation follows her. 203

Enter Claudio and Beatrice, Leonato, Hero.

DON PEDRO	Look, here she comes.
BENEDICK	Will your Grace command me any service to the world's end? I will go on the slightest errand now to the Antipodes that you can devise to send me on; I will fetch you a toothpicker now from the

---

183. **them:** the nestlings. 184. **If...honestly:** If they sing as you say they will, then what you tell me is true; i.e., If I find that you really teach Hero to love Claudio, then I shall know that you are telling me the truth. —**answer:** agree with; accord with. 186. **wrong'd:** slandered. 187. **misus'd:** abused (in her talk). 191. **a great thaw:** At such a time, in Shakespeare's day, the roads were almost or quite impassable and all visiting and festivities were at a standstill; one could only stay at home moping. 191–92. **with such impossible conveyance:** with such superhuman dexterity. —**a man at a mark:** a man set up as a target. 193. **She speaks poniards:** *Poniards* are daggers. 194. **her terminations:** i.e., apparently, the terms that she uses to define or describe one. 195. **to the North Star:** to the ends of the earth. 197. **Hercules:** Hercules, when enslaved to Omphale, wore her clothes while she attired herself in his lion-skin robe and carried his club. Beatrice, says Benedick, would have humiliated him even more than that. 199. **the infernal Ate:** the goddess of discord. 200. **conjure her:** send her home to hell by his exorcisms. 203. **follows her:** attends her wherever she goes.

furthest inch of Asia; bring you the length of Prester John's foot; fetch you a hair off the great Cham's beard; do you any embassage to the Pygmies—rather than hold three words' conference with this harpy. You have no employment for me?   211

DON PEDRO   None, but to desire your good company.

BENEDICK   O God, sir, here's a dish I love not! I cannot endure my Lady Tongue.   *Exit.*

DON PEDRO   Come, lady, come; you have lost the heart of Signior Benedick.

BEATRICE   Indeed, my lord, he lent it me awhile, and I gave him use for it—a double heart for his single one. Marry, once before he won it of me with false dice; therefore your Grace may well say I have lost it.

DON PEDRO   You have put him down, lady; you have put him down.   219

BEATRICE   So I would not he should do me, my lord, lest I should prove the mother of fools. I have brought Count Claudio, whom you sent me to seek.

DON PEDRO   Why, how now, Count? Wherefore are you sad?

CLAUDIO   Not sad, my lord.

DON PEDRO   How then? sick?   225

CLAUDIO   Neither, my lord.

BEATRICE   The Count is neither sad, nor sick, nor merry, nor well; but civil count—civil as an orange, and something of that jealous complexion.   229

DON PEDRO   I' faith, lady, I think your blazon to be true; though I'll be sworn, if he be so, his conceit is false. Here, Claudio, I have wooed in thy name, and fair Hero is won. I have broke with her father, and his good will obtained. Name the day of marriage, and God give thee joy!   234

LEONATO   Count, take of me my daughter, and with her my fortunes. His Grace hath made the match, and all grace say Amen to it!

BEATRICE   Speak, Count, 'tis your cue.

---

208. **Prester John:** A fabled monarch of the Far East, both a King and Christian priest. 209. **the great Cham:** the great Khan of Tartary, ruler of the Mongols. 210. **the Pygmies:** who were supposed to live in the mountains of India. 216. **use:** interest. 226. **Neither:** not sick either. 228. **civil as an orange.** A "Civil orange" was an orange from Civil, i.e., Seville (in Spain). It is bittersweet. 228–29. **of that jealous complexion:** Yellow is the traditional color of jealousy. 230. **your blazon:** your description of him. To *blazon* a coat of arms is to describe it in the technical language of heraldry. 231. **so:** i.e., jealous. **—his conceit is false:** his understanding of the case is incorrect. 236. **all grace say Amen to it!** May all the favor of God confirm it!

CLAUDIO	Silence is the perfectest herald of joy. I were but little happy if I could say how much. Lady, as you are mine, I am yours. I give away myself for you and dote upon the exchange. 240
BEATRICE	Speak, cousin; or, if you cannot, stop his mouth with a kiss and let not him speak neither.
DON PEDRO	In faith, lady, you have a merry heart.
BEATRICE	Yea, my lord; I thank it, poor fool, it keeps on the windy side of care. My cousin tells him in his ear that he is in her heart. 245
CLAUDIO	And so she doth, cousin.
BEATRICE	Good Lord, for alliance! Thus goes every one to the world but I, and I am sun-burnt. I may sit in a corner and cry "Heigh-ho for a husband!"
DON PEDRO	Lady Beatrice, I will get you one. 250
BEATRICE	I would rather have one of your father's getting. Hath your Grace ne'er a brother like you? Your father got excellent husbands, if a maid could come by them.
DON PEDRO	Will you have me, lady?† 254
BEATRICE	No, my lord, unless I might have another for working days: your Grace is too costly to wear every day. But I beseech your Grace pardon me. I was born to speak all mirth and no matter.
DON PEDRO	Your silence most offends me, and to be merry best becomes you, for out o' question you were born in a merry hour. 259
BEATRICE	No, sure, my lord, my mother cried; but then there was a star danc'd, and under that was I born. Cousins, God give you joy!
LEONATO	Niece, will you look to those things I told you of?
BEATRICE	I cry you mercy, uncle. By your Grace's pardon. *Exit.*

---

244. **poor fool:** poor innocent creature. *Fool* is common as a term of affection or compassion. **—on the windy side of care:** to the windward of care (and so not exposed to its blasts). 247. **Good Lord, for alliance!** "Good Lord, how many alliances are forming!" **—goes to the world:** gets married. A common idiom. To *go to the world* is, literally, to abandon the condition of celibacy and take up a "worldly" life. 248. **I am sunburnt:** I am so tanned by the sun that nobody wants to marry me. Only a fair complexion was thought beautiful by the Elizabethan. 251. **getting:** begetting. 252. **got:** begot. 253. **come by:** manage to get. 257. **no matter:** nothing serious or sensible. 258. **offends:** displeases. Much milder in sense than in modern usage. 263. **I cry you mercy:** I beg your pardon for my neglect. **—By your Grace's pardon:** A mere polite farewell, like the modern "Excuse me."

---

†   Don Pedro's proposal is often deeply sincere: both Denzel Washington (Branagh) and Douglas Watson (Antoon) bring to this moment a distinct sense of pathos. The reaction of Beatrice to this proposal often reveals much about her nature. Emma Thompson (Branagh) is clearly moved—and correspondingly sensitive. Kathleen Widdoes (Antoon) gingerly makes light of the proposal. In contrast, both Cherie Lunghi and Jon Finch (Burge) treat the suggestion as light-hearted repartee. [P.K.]

Don Pedro	By my troth, a pleasant-spirited lady.	264

LEONATO   There's little of the melancholy element in her, my lord. She is never sad but when she sleeps, and not ever sad then; for I have heard my daughter say she hath often dreamt of unhappiness and wak'd herself with laughing.

DON PEDRO   She cannot endure to hear tell of a husband.

LEONATO   O, by no means! She mocks all her wooers out of suit.   270

DON PEDRO   She were an excellent wife for Benedick.

LEONATO   O Lord, my lord! if they were but a week married, they would talk themselves mad.

DON PEDRO   County Claudio, when mean you to go to church?   274

CLAUDIO   Tomorrow, my lord. Time goes on crutches till love have all his rites.

LEONATO   Not till Monday, my dear son, which is hence a just sevennight; and a time too brief too, to have all things answer my mind.

DON PEDRO   Come, you shake the head at so long a breathing; but I warrant thee, Claudio, the time shall not go dully by us. I will in the   280 interim undertake one of Hercules' labours, which is, to bring Signior Benedick and the Lady Beatrice into a mountain of affection th' one with th' other. I would fain have it a match, and I doubt not but to fashion it if you three will but minister such assistance as I shall give you direction.   285

LEONATO   My lord, I am for you, though it cost me ten nights' watchings.

CLAUDIO   And I, my lord.

DON PEDRO   And you too, gentle Hero?

HERO   I will do any modest office, my lord, to help my cousin to a good husband.   290

DON PEDRO   And Benedick is not the unhopefullest husband that I know. Thus far can I praise him: he is of a noble strain, of approved valor, and confirm'd honesty. I will teach you how to humor your cousin, that she shall fall in love with Benedick; and I, [to Leonato and

---

267. **unhappiness:** some amusing roguery or other, either in speech or action. 270. **mocks...out of suit:** makes fun of them so that they do not dare to woo her. 277. **son:** Often used by prospective fathers-in-law in old times. —**a just sevennight:** an exact week. 278. **answer my mind:** accord with what I should think fitting for so important an occasion. 279. **breathing:** time to take breath; interval of inaction. 283. **fain:** gladly. 284. **minister:** afford, furnish. 286. **I am for you:** I'm ready to help you in your plan. —**watchings:** keeping awake. 289. **office:** service. 291. **unhopefullest:** least promising. 292. **strain:** lineage, family. —**approved:** tested. 293. **honesty:** honorable character.

Claudio] with your two helps, will so practice on Benedick that, in despite of his quick wit and his queasy stomach, he shall fall in love with Beatrice. If we can do this, Cupid is no longer an archer; his glory shall be ours, for we are the only love-gods. Go in with me, and I will tell you my drift.   *Exeunt.* 299

SCENE II. [*A hall in Leonato's house.*]

Enter [Don] John and Borachio.

DON JOHN   It is so. The Count Claudio shall marry the daughter of Leonato.

BORACHIO   Yea, my lord; but I can cross it.

DON JOHN   Any bar, any cross, any impediment will be med'cinable to me. I am sick in displeasure to him, and whatsoever comes athwart his affection ranges evenly with mine. How canst thou cross this marriage?   6

BORACHIO   Not honestly, my lord, but so covertly that no dishonesty shall appear in me.

DON JOHN   Show me briefly how.

BORACHIO   I think I told your lordship, a year since, how much I am in the favor of Margaret, the waiting gentlewoman to Hero.   11

DON JOHN   I remember.

BORACHIO   I can, at any unseasonable instant of the night, appoint her to look out at her lady's chamber window.

DON JOHN   What life is in that to be the death of this marriage?   15

BORACHIO   The poison of that lies in you to temper. Go you to the Prince your brother; spare not to tell him that he hath wronged his honor in marrying the renowned Claudio (whose estimation do you mightily hold up) to a contaminated stale, such a one as Hero.

DON JOHN   What proof shall I make of that?   20

BORACHIO   Proof enough to misuse the Prince, to vex Claudio, to undo Hero, and kill Leonato. Look you for any other issue?

---

295. **practice on:** work upon him by trickery. A *practice* often means a "plot" or "stratagem." 296. **his queasy stomach:** his delicate digestion—as of one who is very fussy about his fare. 299. **my drift:** my scheme.

SCENE II.
2. **cross it:** thwart the match. 3. **med'cinable to me:** a cure for what ails me. 4. **in displeasure to him:** in my dislike of him. 5. **his affection:** what he likes or wishes. 7. **Not honestly:** not by any honorable means. 8. **in me:** on my part. 13. **appoint her:** arrange with her. 16. **to temper:** to mix, compound. 18. **estimation:** worth. 19. **hold up:** exalt. —**stale:** harlot. 21. **misuse:** delude. —**undo:** ruin.

DON JOHN   Only to despite them I will endeavour anything.

BORACHIO   Go then; find me a meet hour to draw Don Pedro and the Count
Claudio alone; tell them that you know that Hero loves me;   25
intend a kind of zeal both to the Prince and Claudio, as—in
love of your brother's honor, who hath made this match, and
his friend's reputation, who is thus like to be cozen'd with the
semblance of a maid—that you have discover'd thus. They will
scarcely believe this without trial. Offer them instances; which   30
shall bear no less likelihood than to see me at her chamber
window, hear me call Margaret Hero, hear Margaret term me
Claudio; and bring them to see this the very night before the
intended wedding (for in the meantime I will so fashion the
matter that Hero shall be absent) and there shall appear such   35
seeming truth of Hero's disloyalty that jealousy shall be call'd
assurance and all the preparation overthrown.

DON JOHN   Grow this to what adverse issue it can, I will put it in practice. Be
cunning in the working this, and thy fee is a thousand ducats.

BORACHIO   Be you constant in the accusation, and my cunning shall not   40
shame me.

DON JOHN   I will presently go learn their day of marriage.   *Exeunt.*

SCENE III. [*Leonato's orchard.*]

Enter Benedick alone.

BENEDICK   Boy!

[*Enter Boy.*]

BOY   Signior?

BENEDICK   In my chamber window lies a book. Bring it hither to me in the
orchard.

BOY   I am here already, sir.   5

---

23. **Only to despite them:** merely for the sake of doing them an injury. 24. **meet:** fit, convenient. 26.
intend: pretend. 28. **cozen'd with:** cheated by. 30. **without trial:** without testing it. **—instances:**
proofs. 32–33. **term me Claudio:** i.e., in mockery. For Hero to address Borachio as Claudio under
the supposed circumstances would have been as much as to say, "*You* are *my* Claudio! You are the only
Claudio that I care for!" 36. **jealousy:** suspicion. 37. **assurance:** certainty. **—the preparation:** i.e.,
for the marriage. 38. **Grow this...can:** Let this come to whatever evil result is possible. 39. **cunning:**
skilful, clever. **—ducats:** gold coins.

SCENE III.
4. **orchard:** garden. 5. **I am here already:** A conventional phrase for "I will do the errand and return
in an instant."

BENEDICK   I know that, but I would have thee hence and here again. (*Exit Boy.*) I do much wonder that one man, seeing how much another man is a fool when he dedicates his behaviors to love, will, after he hath laugh'd at such shallow follies in others, become the argument of his own scorn by falling in love; and such a man is   9
Claudio. I have known when there was no music with him but the drum and the fife; and now had he rather hear the tabor and the pipe. I have known when he would have walk'd ten mile afoot to see a good armour; and now will he lie ten nights awake carving the fashion of a new doublet. He was wont to speak   15
plain and to the purpose, like an honest man and a soldier; and now is he turn'd orthography; his words are a very fantastical banquet—just so many strange dishes. May I be so converted and see with these eyes? I cannot tell; I think not. I will not be sworn but love may transform me to an oyster; but I'll take my oath   20
on it, till he have made an oyster of me he shall never make me such a fool. One woman is fair, yet I am well; another is wise, yet I am well; another virtuous, yet I am well; but till all graces be in one woman, one woman shall not come in my grace. Rich she shall be, that's certain; wise, or I'll none; virtuous, or I'll never   25
cheapen her; fair, or I'll never look on her; mild, or come not near me; noble, or not I for an angel; of good discourse, an excellent musician, and her hair shall be of what color it please God. Ha, the Prince and Monsieur Love! I will hide me in the arbor.

[*Hides.*]†

Enter Don Pedro, Leonato, Claudio.
Music [*within*].

---

8. **dedicates his behaviors to love:** devotes all his attention to behaving as a lover should. 10. **argument of his own scorn:** the subject of self-contempt. 12–13. **the tabor and the pipe:** the music of social intercourse as opposed to martial music. A tabor is a small drum. 14. **carving:** devising. 15. **doublet:** a kind of jacket. 17. **orthography:** a person who is very fussy and scrupulous about always using the right word and pronouncing it correctly. 19. **with these eyes:** with the eyes of a lover. 23. **graces:** fine qualities. —**be:** are, exist. —**in my grace:** into favor with me. 25. **I'll none:** I'll have nothing to do with her. 26. **cheapen:** bargain for. 27. **noble, or not I for an angel:** She must be of noble birth or I won't take her, even if she is an angel. *Nobles* and *angels* were coins. 28. **of what color it shall please God:** i.e., if these other conditions are satisfied, I will not insist on having her hair of this or that color.

---

† The "gulling" scene, in which Benedick is tricked by his friends into recognizing his love for Beatrice, is one of the centerpieces of the play. In Burge's *Much Ado*, Don Pedro, Leonato and Claudio wander the byways of an orchard as a cynical Benedick shadows them; his transformation is almost feverish. Antoon places Benedick in a row boat, hiding beneath a footbridge as he listens in. Branagh's Benedick is the most comic of the three, fumbling with a folding chair, accidentally shouting in surprise (and pretending his exclamation is the cry of a bird), while his three friends take obvious pleasure in their deceit. In the *Shakespeare Retold* adaptation, the scene takes place on the empty set of the news show. Benedick overhears his friends, who are in the production booth, over an intercom, while they secretly watch his reaction on video monitors. [P.K.]

DON PEDRO	Come, shall we hear this music?	30
CLAUDIO	Yea, my good lord. How still the evening is, As hush'd on purpose to grace harmony!	
DON PEDRO	See you where Benedick hath hid himself?	
CLAUDIO	O, very well, my lord. The music ended, We'll fit the kid-fox with a pennyworth.	35

Enter Balthasar with Music.

DON PEDRO	Come, Balthasar, we'll hear that song again.	
BALTHASAR	O, good my lord, tax not so bad a voice To slander music any more than once.	
DON PEDRO	It is the witness still of excellency To put a strange face on his own perfection. I pray thee sing, and let me woo no more.	40
BALTHASAR	Because you talk of wooing, I will sing, Since many a wooer doth commence his suit To her he thinks not worthy, yet he wooes, Yet will he swear he loves.	
DON PEDRO	Nay, pray thee come; Or if thou wilt hold longer argument, Do it in notes.	45
BALTHASAR	Note this before my notes: There's not a note of mine that's worth the noting.	
DON PEDRO	Why, these are very crotchets that he speaks! Note notes, forsooth, and nothing!	*[Music.]* 50
BENEDICK	*[aside]* Now divine air! Now is his soul ravish'd! Is it not strange that sheep's guts should hale souls out of men's bodies? Well, a horn for my money, when all's done. *[Balthasar sings.]*	

The Song.

---

32. **to grace harmony:** to do honor to the music. 35. **We'll fit the kid-fox with a pennyworth:** We'll give the sly young fellow good payment for eavesdropping; he shall hear more than he bargained for. 37. **tax not:** task not. 39. **the witness:** evidence. —**still:** always. 40. **To put a strange face on his own perfection:** to pretend not to recognize its own perfection. 41. **let me woo no more:** do not make me coax you any longer. 46. **argument:** talk. 49. **crotchets:** A pun, as usual: (1) "he actually talks in musical notes" (a crotchet being a quarter note); (2) "he uses punning tricks" —"whimsical turns of phrase." 50. **Note…nothing!** Thus Don Pedro repeats Balthasar's mock-modest remark and comments on it. "Upon my word, he actually talks of 'noting notes' and 'noting' —and it all amounts to *nothing!*" *Nothing* was almost or quite identical in pronunciation with *noting*. It rhymes with *doting*. 51. **Now divine air!** Now, I suppose, Don Pedro is ready to call this tune "divine"! Benedick pretends to be insensible to the charm of music. 52. **hale:** draw. 53. **a horn:** a hunting horn—something more masculine than these stringed instruments! —**when all's done:** after all.

> Sigh no more, ladies, sigh no more!
> Men were deceivers ever,   55
> One foot in sea, and one on shore;
> To one thing constant never.
> Then sigh not so,
> But let them go,
> And be you blithe and bonny,   60
> Converting all your sounds of woe
> Into Hey nonny, nonny.
> Sing no more ditties, sing no moe,
> Of dumps so dull and heavy!
> The fraud of men was ever so,   65
> Since summer first was leavy.
> Then sigh not so, &c.

DON PEDRO   By my troth, a good song.

BALTHASAR   And an ill singer, my lord.

DON PEDRO   Ha, no, no faith! Thou sing'st well enough for a shift.   70

BENEDICK   [aside] An he had been a dog that should have howl'd thus, they
              would have hang'd him; and I pray God his bad voice bode no
              mischief. I had as lief have heard the night raven, come what
              plague could have come after it.

DON PEDRO   Yea, marry. Dost thou hear, Balthasar? I pray thee get us some   75
              excellent music; for tomorrow night we would have it at the Lady
              Hero's chamber window.

BALTHASAR   The best I can, my lord.

DON PEDRO   Do so. Farewell.   Exit Balthasar [with Musicians].
              Come hither, Leonato. What was it you told me of today? that   80
              your niece Beatrice was in love with Signior Benedick?

CLAUDIO   O, ay!—[Aside to Pedro] Stalk on, stalk on; the fowl sits.—I did
              never think that lady would have loved any man.

LEONATO   No, nor I neither; but most wonderful that she should so dote on
              Signior Benedick, whom she hath in all outward behaviors seem'd
              ever to abhor.   86

BENEDICK   [aside] Is't possible? Sits the wind in that corner?

---

60. **bonny:** cheerful. 62. **Hey nonny, nonny:** A cheerful refrain. 63. **moe:** more. 64. **dumps:** sorrowful
moods. —**heavy:** mournful. 65. **ever so:** always just as it is now. 65. **leavy:** leafy. 70. **for a shift:** for an
emergency. 72–73. **bode no mischief:** be not a portent of misfortune—like the howling of a dog in the
night. —**as lief:** as willingly. —**the night raven:** The croaking of a raven was thought to be ominous,
especially in the night. 75. **Yea, marry:** Yes, to be sure. 82. **Stalk on...the fowl sits:** Go on quietly; the
bird has landed and now is the time to catch him! 87. **Sits...corner?** Is *that* the way the wind blows?

LEONATO	By my troth, my lord, I cannot tell what to think of it, but that she loves him with an enraged affection. It is past the infinite of thought. 90
DON PEDRO	May be she doth but counterfeit.
CLAUDIO	Faith, like enough.
LEONATO	O God, counterfeit? There was never counterfeit of passion came so near the life of passion as she discovers it.
DON PEDRO	Why, what effects of passion shows she? 95
CLAUDIO	[*aside*] Bait the hook well! This fish will bite.
LEONATO	What effects, my lord? She will sit you—you heard my daughter tell you how.
CLAUDIO	She did indeed.
DON PEDRO	How, how, I pray you? You amaze me. I would have thought her spirit had been invincible against all assaults of affection. 101
LEONATO	I would have sworn it had, my lord—especially against Benedick.
BENEDICK	[*aside*] I should think this a gull but that the white-bearded fellow speaks it. Knavery cannot, sure, hide himself in such reverence.
CLAUDIO	[*aside*] He hath ta'en th' infection. Hold it up. 105
DON PEDRO	Hath she made her affection known to Benedick?
LEONATO	No, and swears she never will. That's her torment.
CLAUDIO	'Tis true indeed. So your daughter says. "Shall I," says she, "that have so oft encount'red him with scorn, write to him that I love him?" 110
LEONATO	This says she now when she is beginning to write to him; for she'll be up twenty times a night, and there will she sit in her smock till she have writ a sheet of paper. My daughter tells us all.
CLAUDIO	Now you talk of a sheet of paper, I remember a pretty jest your daughter told us of. 115
LEONATO	O, when she had writ it, and was reading it over, she found "Benedick" and "Beatrice" between the sheet?
CLAUDIO	That.

---

89. **enraged:** madly passionate. 89–90. **past…thought:** Thought can go infinitely beyond facts, but this love of hers is greater even than thought can imagine. 94. **discovers:** reveals, shows. 95. **effects:** outward signs. 97. **sit you:** sit (a colloquialism) Leonato continues this thought at line 112. 103. **a gull:** a hoax. 105. **Hold it up:** Keep it up. 109. **encount'red him with scorn:** matched him in contemptuous skirmishing. 117. **between the sheet:** in the folded sheet of paper. 118. **That:** Yes, that's the one I meant.

Leonato	O, she tore the letter into a thousand halfpence, rail'd at herself that she should be so immodest to write to one that she knew 120 would flout her. "I measure him," says she, "by my own spirit; for I should flout him if he writ to me. Yea, though I love him, I should."
Claudio	Then down upon her knees she falls, weeps, sobs, beats her heart, tears her hair, prays, curses—"O sweet Benedick! God give me patience!" 126
Leonato	She doth indeed; my daughter says so. And the ecstasy hath so much overborne her that my daughter is sometime afeard she will do a desperate outrage to herself. It is very true.
Don Pedro	It were good that Benedick knew of it by some other, if she will not discover it. 131
Claudio	To what end? He would make but a sport of it and torment the poor lady worse.
Don Pedro	An he should, it were an alms to hang him! She's an excellent sweet lady, and (out of all suspicion) she is virtuous. 135
Claudio	And she is exceeding wise.
Don Pedro	In everything but in loving Benedick.
Leonato	O, my lord, wisdom and blood combating in so tender a body, we have ten proofs to one that blood hath the victory. I am sorry for her, as I have just cause, being her uncle and her guardian. 140
Don Pedro	I would she had bestowed this dotage on me. I would have daff'd all other respects and made her half myself. I pray you tell Benedick of it and hear what 'a will say.
Leonato	Were it good, think you? 144
Claudio	Hero thinks surely she will die; for she says she will die if he love her not, and she will die ere she make her love known, and she will die, if he woo her, rather than she will bate one breath of her accustomed crossness.
Don Pedro	She doth well. If she should make tender of her love, 'tis very possible he'll scorn it; for the man (as you know all) hath a 150 contemptible spirit.

---

121. **flout:** mock. 127. **ecstasy:** madness. 128. **overborne:** overcome. 131. **discover it:** reveal it to him. 134. **an alms:** a deed of charity. 134–35. **excellent sweet:** very charming. 138. **blood:** natural impulse—almost equivalent to "human nature." 139. **proofs:** examples, instances. 141. **dotage:** doting affection. 142. **daff'd all other respects:** put aside (disregarded) all other considerations. 145. **will die:** is resolved to die. 147. **bate:** abate, give up. 148. **crossness:** perversity, contrariety. 149. **make tender:** make him an offer. 151. **contemptible:** contemptuous, scornful.

CLAUDIO	He is a very proper man.
DON PEDRO	He hath indeed a good outward happiness.
CLAUDIO	Before God! and in my mind, very wise.
DON PEDRO	He doth indeed show some sparks that are like wit. 155
CLAUDIO	And I take him to be valiant.
DON PEDRO	As Hector, I assure you; and in the managing of quarrels you may say he is wise, for either he avoids them with great discretion, or undertakes them with a most Christianlike fear. 159
LEONATO	If he do fear God, 'a must necessarily keep peace. If he break the peace, he ought to enter into a quarrel with fear and trembling.
DON PEDRO	And so will he do; for the man doth fear God, howsoever it seems not in him by some large jests he will make. Well, I am sorry for your niece. Shall we go seek Benedick and tell him of her love?
CLAUDIO	Never tell him, my lord. Let her wear it out with good counsel. 165
LEONATO	Nay, that's impossible; she may wear her heart out first.
DON PEDRO	Well, we will hear further of it by your daughter. Let it cool the while. I love Benedick well, and I could wish he would modestly examine himself to see how much he is unworthy so good a lady.
LEONATO	My lord, will you walk? Dinner is ready. [*They walk away.*] 170
CLAUDIO	If he do not dote on her upon this, I will never trust my expectation.
DON PEDRO	Let there be the same net spread for her, and that must your daughter and her gentlewomen carry. The sport will be, when they hold one an opinion of another's dotage, and no such matter. That's the scene that I would see, which will be merely a dumb show. Let us send her to call him in to dinner. 177

Exeunt [Don Pedro, Claudio, and Leonato].

[Benedick advances from the arbor.]

| BENEDICK | This can be no trick. The conference was sadly borne; they have the truth of this from Hero; they seem to pity the lady. It seems her affections have their full bent. Love me? Why, it must be   180 |

---

152. **proper:** handsome. 153. **a good outward happiness:** an attractive exterior. 155. **wit:** intelligence, mental alertness. 163. **by:** to judge by. —**large:** broad, indecorous. 165. **wear it out with good counsel:** work out her own cure by considering what is best for herself. 171. **upon this:** as a result of this talk of ours (which he has overheard). 174. **carry:** manage. 174–75. **when they hold...dotage:** when each thinks that the other is in love. —**and no such matter:** and yet that is not the case. 176. **merely:** purely; out and out. 176–77. **a dumb show:** a piece of action without words, like a pantomime. 178. **sadly borne:** carried on seriously—in earnest. 180. **affections:** feelings of affection. —**have their full bent:** are intense in the highest degree. The figure comes from *bending* a bow.

requited. I hear how I am censur'd. They say I will bear myself proudly if I perceive the love come from her. They say too that she will rather die than give any sign of affection. I did never think to marry. I must not seem proud. Happy are they that hear their detractions and can put them to mending. They say the lady is fair—'tis a truth, I can bear them witness; and virtuous—'tis so, I cannot reprove it; and wise, but for loving me—by my troth, it is no addition to her wit, nor no great argument of her folly, for I will be horribly in love with her. I may chance have some odd quirks and remnants of wit broken on me because I have railed so long against marriage. But doth not the appetite alter? A man loves the meat in his youth that he cannot endure in his age. Shall quips and sentences and these paper bullets of the brain awe a man from the career of his humor? No, the world must be peopled. When I said I would die a bachelor, I did not think I should live till I were married.   196

Enter Beatrice.

Here comes Beatrice. By this day, she's a fair lady! I do spy some marks of love in her.

BEATRICE   Against my will I am sent to bid you come in to dinner.

BENEDICK   Fair Beatrice, I thank you for your pains.   200

BEATRICE   I took no more pains for those thanks than you take pains to thank me. If it had been painful, I would not have come.

BENEDICK   You take pleasure then in the message?

BEATRICE   Yea, just so much as you may take upon a knive's point, and choke a daw withal. You have no stomach, signior. Fare you well.   205

Exit.

BENEDICK   Ha! "Against my will I am sent to bid you come in to dinner." There's a double meaning in that. "I took no more pains for those thanks than you took pains to thank me." That's as much as to say, "Any pains that I take for you is as easy as thanks." If I do not take pity of her, I am a villain; if I do not love her, I am a Jew. I will go get her picture.   *Exit.* 211

---

181. **censur'd:** judged. 184–85. **hear their own detractions:** hear themselves censured for their faults. —**can put them to mending:** can undertake to cure themselves of those faults. 187. **reprove:** disprove, confute. 189–90. **some odd quirks and remnants:** some few tricks of phrase and old fragments of wit. 192. **meat:** food. 193. **quips:** mocking remarks. —**sentences:** wise sayings. 193–94. **awe…humor:** frighten a man from the course of action that his fancy prompts. 205. **a daw:** a jackdaw —proverbially a stupid bird. Beatrice implies that she should be silly to take pleasure in doing Benedick a favor. —**withal:** with it. —**stomach:** appetite. 210. **a Jew:** lacking charity—a stereotype in Shakespeare's day.

ACT III

SCENE I. [*Leonato's orchard.*]

Enter Hero and two Gentlewomen, Margaret and Ursula.

HERO   Good Margaret, run thee to the parlor.
            There shalt thou find my cousin Beatrice
            Proposing with the Prince and Claudio.
            Whisper her ear and tell her, I and Ursley
            Walk in the orchard, and our whole discourse   5
            Is all of her. Say that thou overheard'st us;
            And bid her steal into the pleached bower,
            Where honeysuckles, ripened by the sun,
            Forbid the sun to enter—like favorites,
            Made proud by princes, that advance their pride   10
            Against that power that bred it. There will she hide her
            To listen our propose. This is thy office.
            Bear thee well in it and leave us alone.

MARGARET   I'll make her come, I warrant you, presently.   [*Exit.*]

HERO   Now, Ursula, when Beatrice doth come,   15
            As we do trace this alley up and down,
            Our talk must only be of Benedick.
            When I do name him, let it be thy part
            To praise him more than ever man did merit.
            My talk to thee must be how Benedick   20
            Is sick in love with Beatrice. Of this matter
            Is little Cupid's crafty arrow made,
            That only wounds by hearsay.

                        Enter Beatrice.

                                        Now begin;
            For look where Beatrice like a lapwing runs
            Close by the ground, to hear our conference.   25

ACT III. SCENE I.
3. **Proposing:** talking, conversing. 10–11. **advance their pride...bred it:** carry their arrogance to such a height that they rebel against the ruler whose favor made them great. *Advance* means "raise." 12. **propose:** talk. —**thy office:** thy part in the affair. 13. **Bear thee well:** carry thyself well; play thy part well. 14. **presently:** immediately. 16. **trace this alley:** stroll at a leisurely pace along this walk. 21. **Of this matter:** of such material as will make up this conversation. 22. **crafty arrow:** i.e., the arrow that Cupid will choose in this particular case. 24. **lapwing:** a bird that scurries along the ground.

[Beatrice hides in the arbor.]†

 URSULA   The pleasant'st angling is to see the fish
          Cut with her golden oars the silver stream
          And greedily devour the treacherous bait.
          So angle we for Beatrice, who even now
          Is couched in the woodbine coverture.   30
          Fear you not my part of the dialogue.

HERO   Then go we near her, that her ear lose nothing
          Of the false sweet bait that we lay for it.
                                    [They approach the arbor.]
          No, truly, Ursula, she is too disdainful.
          I know her spirits are as coy and wild   35
          As haggards of the rock.

URSULA   But are you sure
          That Benedick loves Beatrice so entirely?

HERO   So says the Prince, and my newtrothed lord.

URSULA   And did they bid you tell her of it, madam?

HERO   They did entreat me to acquaint her of it;   40
          But I persuaded them, if they lov'd Benedick,
          To wish him wrestle with affection
          And never to let Beatrice know of it.

URSULA   Why did you so? Doth not the gentleman
          Deserve as full, as fortunate a bed   45
          As ever Beatrice shall couch upon?

HERO   O god of love! I know he doth deserve
          As much as may be yielded to a man;
          But Nature never fram'd a woman's heart
          Of prouder stuff than that of Beatrice.   50
          Disdain and scorn ride sparkling in her eyes,
          Misprizing what they look on; and her wit
          Values itself so highly that to her

---

30. **couched:** hidden. —**woodbine coverture:** bower of honeysuckle. 36. **haggards:** wild hawks. 42. **To wish him wrestle:** to advise him to wrestle. 44–46. **Doth not...upon?** Does Benedick not deserve as much prosperity and happiness in marriage as a match with Beatrice would bring him? 48. **may be yielded:** can be granted. 52. **Misprizing:** despising, undervaluing.

---

†   Beatrice's gulling scene mirrors that of Benedick (2.3). In the BBC version, Beatrice is visibly
     distressed, yet almost motionless, as she listens to the ladies criticize her in the arbor; her reaction
     is measured, yet clearly passionate. Both Antoon and Branagh follow stage tradition in having
     Beatrice comically flutter about like a "lapwing" as she eavesdrops. In Antoon's version, set in a
     glasshouse, Beatrice is caught in the spray of a sprinkler that Hero turns on surreptitiously. [P.K.]

All matter else seems weak. She cannot love,
Nor take no shape nor project of affection,   55
She is so self-endeared.

URSULA   Sure I think so;
And therefore certainly it were not good
She knew his love, lest she'll make sport at it.

HERO   Why, you speak truth. I never yet saw man,
How wise, how noble, young, how rarely featur'd,   60
But she would spell him backward. If fair-fac'd,
She would swear the gentleman should be her sister;
If black, why, Nature, drawing of an antic,
Made a foul blot; if tall, a lance ill-headed;
If low, an agate very vilely cut;   65
If speaking, why, a vane blown with all winds;
If silent, why, a block moved with none.
So turns she every man the wrong side out
And never gives to truth and virtue that
Which simpleness and merit purchaseth.   70

URSULA   Sure, sure, such carping is not commendable.

HERO   No, not to be so odd, and from all fashions,
As Beatrice is, cannot be commendable.
But who dare tell her so? If I should speak,
She would mock me into air; O, she would laugh me   75
Out of myself, press me to death with wit!
Therefore let Benedick, like cover'd fire,
Consume away in sighs, waste inwardly.
It were a better death than die with mocks,
Which is as bad as die with tickling.   80

URSULA   Yet tell her of it. Hear what she will say.

HERO   No; rather I will go to Benedick
And counsel him to fight against his passion.

---

54. **All matter else seems weak:** All subjects seem trivial to her except her own clever ideas and witty speeches. 55. **Nor...affection:** nor form in her mind any clear conception—or, indeed, even a vague idea—of what love is. 60. **rarely featur'd:** beautiful in face and form. 61. **spell him backward:** turn all his good points into defects. 63. **black:** of dark complexion. 63–64. **drawing...blot:** in trying to draw a comic figure, succeeded only in making an ugly and shapeless one. 65. **an agate:** a tiny figure cut in the agate set in a ring. 70. **purchaseth:** deserve. 71. **carping:** faultfinding. 72. **No, not...commendable:** No, not to be so odd and so eccentric as Beatrice is—*that,* as you say, cannot be regarded as praiseworthy. —**from all fashions.** This phrase repeats and emphasizes the meaning of *odd. From* is emphatic: "away from," "out of harmony with," "contrary to." 76. **press me to death.** Pressing to death by laying heavy weights upon the body was the regular English penalty for "standing mute," i.e., for refusing to plead "guilty" or "not guilty" when accused of felony. 78. **waste inwardly.** Every sigh was said to draw a drop of blood from the heart.

	And truly, I'll devise some honest slanders	
	To stain my cousin with. One doth not know	85
	How much an ill word may empoison liking.	

URSULA   O, do not do your cousin such a wrong!
She cannot be so much without true judgment
(Having so swift and excellent a wit
As she is priz'd to have) as to refuse   90
So rare a gentleman as Signior Benedick.

HERO   He is the only man of Italy,
Always excepted my dear Claudio.

URSULA   I pray you be not angry with me, madam,
Speaking my fancy: Signior Benedick,   95
For shape, for bearing, argument, and valor,
Goes foremost in report through Italy.

HERO   Indeed he hath an excellent good name.

URSULA   His excellence did earn it ere he had it.
When are you married, madam?   100

HERO   Why, every day tomorrow! Come, go in.
I'll show thee some attires, and have thy counsel
Which is the best to furnish me tomorrow.   [*They walk away.*]

URSULA   She's lim'd, I warrant you! We have caught her, madam.

HERO   If it prove so, then loving goes by haps;   105
Some Cupid kills with arrows, some with traps.

                         Exeunt [*Hero and Ursula*].

         [*Beatrice advances from the arbor.*]

BEATRICE   What fire is in mine ears? Can this be true?
Stand I condemn'd for pride and scorn so much?
Contempt, farewell! and maiden pride, adieu!
No glory lives behind the back of such.   110
And, Benedick, love on; I will requite thee,
Taming my wild heart to thy loving hand.

---

84. **honest:** honorable—i.e., not inconsistent with chastity. 90. **priz'd to have:** credited with having. 92. **the only man:** the very best man. *Only* is used to express unique excellence. 96. **bearing:** manner. **—argument:** discourse—not "discussion" but "style in talk," "ability to sustain his part in conversation." 101. **Why, every day tomorrow!** Why, I shall be a married woman every day of my life after tomorrow's wedding! Hero's reply twists the sense of Ursula's question. 103. **furnish me:** dress me with. 104. **lim'd:** caught as with birdlime—a sticky substance smeared upon twigs to catch birds. 105. **by haps:** merely by luck and chance. 107. **What fire is in mine ears?** What makes my ears burn so? An allusion to the old saying that, when our ears burn, it is a sign that somebody, somewhere, is talking about us —and not always to our credit. 110. **No glory lives behind the back of such:** No one will praise such a proud person when they are not present (i.e., behind their back) [P.K.].

If thou dost love, my kindness shall incite thee
To bind our loves up in a holy band;
For others say thou dost deserve, and I   115
Believe it better than reportingly.   *Exit.*

SCENE II. [*A room in Leonato's house.*]

Enter Don Pedro, Claudio, Benedick, and Leonato.

DON PEDRO   I do but stay till your marriage be consummate, and then go I
toward Arragon.

CLAUDIO   I'll bring you thither, my lord, if you'll vouchsafe me.

DON PEDRO   Nay, that would be as great a soil in the new gloss of your marriage
as to show a child his new coat and forbid him to wear it. I will   5
only be bold with Benedick for his company; for, from the crown
of his head to the sole of his foot, he is all mirth. He hath twice
or thrice cut Cupid's bowstring, and the little hangman dare not
shoot at him. He hath a heart as sound as a bell; and his tongue is
the clapper, for what his heart thinks, his tongue speaks.   10

BENEDICK   Gallants, I am not as I have been.

LEONATO   So say I. Methinks you are sadder.

CLAUDIO   I hope he be in love.

DON PEDRO   Hang him, truant! There's no true drop of blood in him to be truly
touch'd with love. If he be sad, he wants money.   15

BENEDICK   I have the toothache.

DON PEDRO   Draw it.

BENEDICK   Hang it!

CLAUDIO   You must hang it first and draw it afterwards.

---

116. **Believe it better than reportingly:** give more credit to it than one gives to mere report. Beatrice
thus reveals to the audience that she has always thought well of Benedick in spite of her gibes.
SCENE II.
1. **consummate:** consummated, accomplished. 3. **bring you:** escort you; go with you as an attendant.
—**vouchsafe me:** allow me. 6. **be bold with...company:** take the liberty of asking Benedick to give
me the pleasure of his society. 8. **hangman:** rascal. 12. **sadder:** more serious, not more sorrowful.
14. **truant:** inconstant fellow. 17. **Draw.** The regular old word for *extracting* a tooth. Since to "draw"
meant also to "eviscerate" —*hanging, drawing,* and *quartering* being the regular punishment for traitors
—Don Pedro's "draw" suggests hanging, and Benedick curses his tooth with a "Hang it!" This reminds
Claudio of the teeth he has seen hung up as signs in the shop windows of barbers (the dentists of those
days), and he remarks that, whereas in the regular course of events a tooth had to be drawn before it was
hung up, Benedick should follow the executioner's practice —hang the culprit first and then draw him.

Don Pedro	What? sigh for the toothache?	20
Leonato	Where is but a humor or a worm.	
Benedick	Well, every one can master a grief but he that has it.	
Claudio	Yet say I he is in love.	
Don Pedro	There is no appearance of fancy in him, unless it be a fancy that he hath to strange disguises; as to be a Dutchman today, a Frenchman tomorrow; or in the shape of two countries at once, as a German from the waist downward, all slops, and a Spaniard from the hip upward, no doubtlet. Unless he have a fancy to this foolery, as it appears he hath, he is no fool for fancy, as you would have it appear he is.	25 / 30
Claudio	If he be not in love with some woman, there is no believing old signs. 'A brushes his hat o' mornings. What should that bode?†	
Don Pedro	Hath any man seen him at the barber's?	
Claudio	No, but the barber's man hath been seen with him, and the old ornament of his cheek hath already stuff'd tennis balls.	35
Leonato	Indeed he looks younger than he did, by the loss of a beard.	
Don Pedro	Nay, 'a rubs himself with civet. Can you smell him out by that?	
Claudio	That's as much as to say, the sweet youth's in love.	
Don Pedro	The greatest note of it is his melancholy.	
Claudio	And when was he wont to wash his face?	40
Don Pedro	Yea, or to paint himself? for the which I hear what they say of him.	
Claudio	Nay, but his jesting spirit, which is new-crept into a lute string, and now govern'd by stops.	
Don Pedro	Indeed that tells a heavy tale for him. Conclude, conclude, he is in love.	45

---

21. **humor:** a morbid secretion. 24. **fancy:** love. 27. **slops:** loose breeches. 28. **doublet:** a close-fitting jacket. Long cloaks were the fashion in Spain. 29. **no fool for fancy:** not befooled by love; no victim of love. 32. **bode:** portend, signify. 35. **stuff'd tennis balls.** As a soldier, Benedick was heavily bearded when he returned from the campaign. 37. **civet.** A favorite perfume in old times. It comes from the civet cat. 39. **note:** mark, sign. 40. **wash his face:** i.e., with cosmetics. 41. **for the which:** with reference to which. 43. **which is new-crept into a lute string:** which is recently changed to a tune of love. 44. **govern'd by stops:** so controlled by his love that it does not run without restraint. *Stops* or "frets" are small bars of wire or wood on a musical instrument to guide the fingering by indicating the division into notes. 45. **heavy:** sorrowful.

---

†   In this scene, Benedick is seen clean-shaven for the first time, taking much greater care with his grooming and dress than he has ever before. This is a sign, his friends note, of a man in love. In 2.3, Benedick mocked Claudio for just such a transformation. [P.K.]

Claudio	Nay, but I know who loves him.
Don Pedro	That would I know too. I warrant, one that knows him not.
Claudio	Yes, and his ill conditions; and in despite of all, dies for him.
Don Pedro	She shall be buried with her face upwards. 50
Benedick	Yet is this no charm for the toothache. Old signior, walk aside with me. I have studied eight or nine wise words to speak to you, which these hobby-horses must not hear.

[Exeunt Benedick and Leonato.]

Don Pedro	For my life, to break with him about Beatrice! 55
Claudio	'Tis even so. Hero and Margaret have by this played their parts with Beatrice, and then the two bears will not bite one another when they meet.

Enter John the Bastard.

Don John	My lord and brother, God save you,
Don Pedro	Good den, brother. 60
Don John	If your leisure serv'd, I would speak with you.
Don Pedro	In private?
Don John	If it please you. Yet Count Claudio may hear, for what I would speak of concerns him.
Don Pedro	What's the matter? 65
Don John	[*to Claudio*] Means your lordship to be married tomorrow?
Don Pedro	You know he does.
Don John	I know not that, when he knows what I know.
Claudio	If there be any impediment, I pray you discover it. 69
Don John	You may think I love you not. Let that appear hereafter, and aim better at me by that I now will manifest. For my brother, I think

---

49. **conditions:** traits of character. 50. **face upwards:** suicides were buried face downwards, but dying of love would not be Beatrice's fault. 51. **Yet is this no charm for the toothache:** Yet all this idle talk of yours provides no magic spell to cure my toothache—that is just as bad as ever it was. 53. **hobby-horses:** silly jokers. The hobby-horse was a ludicrous character in the old May games and morris dances. 55. **For my life:** I'll bet my life on it. 56. **Margaret:** It was Ursula who joined Hero in playing the trick on Beatrice, but Margaret also had an important share in the game. 57. **the two bears:** There is a humorous suggestion that Benedick and Beatrice are unnaturally savage, for it is an old saying that "one bear will not bite another." 60. **Good den:** good e'en—i.e., good even; good afternoon. The regular greeting after midday. 65. **the matter:** the subject matter—that about which you wish to speak with me. 69. **discover:** disclose. 70. **that:** the question whether I am your friend or not. 70–71. **aim better at me:** have a better understanding of my feelings toward you.

he holds you well and in dearness of heart hath holp to effect your ensuing marriage—surely suit ill spent and labour ill bestowed!

DON PEDRO   Why, what's the matter?   74

DON JOHN   I came hither to tell you, and, circumstances short'ned (for she has been too long a-talking of), the lady is disloyal.

CLAUDIO   Who? Hero?

DON JOHN   Even she—Leonato's Hero, your Hero, every man's Hero.

CLAUDIO   Disloyal?

DON JOHN   The word is too good to paint out her wickedness. I could say   80
she were worse: think you of a worse title, and I will fit her to it. Wonder not till further warrant. Go but with me tonight, you shall see her chamber window ent'red, even the night before her wedding day. If you love her then, tomorrow wed her. But it would better fit your honor to change your mind.   85

CLAUDIO   May this be so?

DON PEDRO   I will not think it.

DON JOHN   If you dare not trust that you see, confess not that you know. If you will follow me, I will show you enough; and when you have seen more and heard more, proceed accordingly.   90

CLAUDIO   If I see anything tonight why I should not marry her tomorrow, in the congregation where I should wed, there will I shame her.

DON PEDRO   And, as I wooed for thee to obtain her, I will join with thee to disgrace her.

DON JOHN   I will disparage her no farther till you are my witnesses. Bear it coldly but till midnight, and let the issue show itself.   96

DON PEDRO   O day untowardly turned!

CLAUDIO   O mischief strangely thwarting!

---

72. **holds you well:** thinks well of you. **—in dearness of heart:** in heartfelt friendship. **—holp:** helped. 73. **bestowed:** spent, used. 74. **Why,...matter?** Don Pedro repeats his question, impatient at Don John's delay in answering it. 75. **circumstances short'ned:** to cut short all talk about matters of detail. 75–76. **she...a-talking of:** we have spent more time in talking about her than she deserves. 80. **to paint out:** to describe in full. 82. **till further warrant:** until you have further evidence to confirm my words. 88. **If you dare not...know:** If you have not strength of mind enough to believe your eyes, then do not admit the truth of what you know. When I show you the truth, either recognize it, or deny your knowledge of plain facts. 95. **till you are my witnesses:** until you can confirm my evidence. 95–96. **Bear it coldly:** Keep cool about the matter. **—let...itself:** let the result of your observation serve as a proof of the fact. 97. **untowardly turned:** changed from a day of joy to a day of sorrow. 98. **mischief strangely thwarting:** misfortune strangely destructive of my hopes of happiness.

DON JOHN   O plague right well prevented!
             So will you say when you have seen the sequel.   *Exeunt.*† 100

SCENE III. [*A street.*]

Enter Dogberry and his compartner [Verges], with the Watch.‡

DOGBERRY   Are you good men and true?

VERGES   Yea, or else it were pity but they should suffer salvation, body and
             soul.

DOGBERRY   Nay, that were a punishment too good for them if they should
             have any allegiance in them, being chosen for the Prince's watch.

VERGES   Well, give them their charge, neighbor Dogberry.   6

DOGBERRY   First, who think you the most desartless man to be constable?

1. WATCH   Hugh Oatcake, sir, or George Seacoal; for they can write and read.

DOGBERRY   Come hither, neighbor Seacoal. God hath bless'd you with a good
             name. To be a well-favored man is the gift of fortune, but to write
             and read comes by nature.   11

2. WATCH   Both which, Master Constable—

---

99. **plague:** misfortune. —**prevented:** headed off in advance; forestalled. *Prevent* in Shakespeare always
keeps the force of *pre-*.
SCENE III.
Dogberry is Head Constable. Verges is Headborough—a constable of somewhat lower rank. In the stage
direction he is called Dogberry's "compartner," i.e., copartner, associate. 1. **true:** loyal. 2. **salvation.**
The trick of making a person say the opposite of what he means is carried very far in this scene. In at
least one instance—"tolerable, and not to be endured"—the blunder is so exquisite that posterity has
adopted it as a kind of proverb. Dogberry and Verges are caricatures: actual officers of Shakespeare's
time may have been quite as absurd, but they cannot possibly have been so amusing. Shakespeare's
creative power has made caricatures become characters. 5. **any allegiance.** Dogberry means "lack of
allegiance." 6. **give them their charge:** inform them what their duties are. 7. **desartless:** deserving. —
constable: chief watchman. 9–10. **a good name.** Doubtless Dogberry means "a good reputation," but
he seems to be congratulating Seacoal on the beauty of his family name! —**well-favored:** handsome.

---

†   Although the scene in which Margaret impersonates Hero at her window is not enacted in
     Shakespeare's play, Branagh chooses to enact it, as do some stage productions. He felt that this would
     increase our sympathy for Claudio, allowing us to forgive him at the end, as Hero seemingly does. In
     the *Shakespeare Retold* version, Don shows Claude photos of Hero, on the back of which he has forged
     love notes from her to him, as well as text messages he has faked. He then connives to have Claude see
     him enter Hero's room the night before her wedding; when Claude calls Hero on her cell phone, she
     naively tells him that she is alone, to cover for Don's inappropriate appearance in her room. [P.K.]

‡   In the BBC *Much Ado*, Dogberry is large, blustery, yet genial, as he commands his crew preparing
     for their watch in a dark, arched alleyway. Michael Keaton's Dogberry (Branagh) is strikingly
     different: he is unkempt and greasy, sadistically prodding and slapping Verges and the watch as he
     orders them about. [P.K.]

In keeping with the theme of small-town Americana, and playing with the conventions of early American cinema, Antoon casts Dogberry and the Watch as Keystone Cops. 919730

DOGBERRY	You have. I knew it would be your answer. Well, for your favor, sir, why, give God thanks and make no boast of it; and for your writing and reading, let that appear when there is no need of 15 such vanity. You are thought here to be the most senseless and fit man for the constable of the watch. Therefore bear you the lanthorn. This is your charge: you shall comprehend all vagrom men; you are to bid any man stand, in the Prince's name.
2. WATCH	How if 'a will not stand? 20
DOGBERRY	Why then, take no note of him, but let him go, and presently call the rest of the watch together and thank God you are rid of a knave.
VERGES	If he will not stand when he is bidden, he is none of the Prince's subjects. 25
DOGBERRY	True, and they are to meddle with none but the Prince's subjects. You shall also make no noise in the streets; for for the watch to babble and to talk is most tolerable, and not to be endured.

13. **for your favor:** as for your features. 16. **such vanity:** such a piece of showy frivolity. But perhaps Dogberry means "such a valuable accomplishment." 18. **lanthorn.** An old form of *lantern,* probably due to the fact that lanterns were often made of a thin sheet of horn. —**comprehend:** for *apprehend;* i.e., "arrest." —**vagrom:** vagrant. Dogberry means merely "strangers wandering about the streets." 24. **none:** Emphatic: "certainly not one." 26. **meddle:** concern themselves; have to do.

2. WATCH	We will rather sleep than talk. We know what belongs to a watch.
DOGBERRY	Why, you speak like an ancient and most quiet watchman, for I 30 cannot see how sleeping should offend. Only have a care that your bills be not stol'n. Well, you are to call at all the alehouses and bid those that are drunk get them to bed.
2. WATCH	How if they will not?
DOGBERRY	Why then, let them alone till they are sober. If they make you 35 not then the better answer, you may say they are not the men you took them for.
2. WATCH	Well, sir.
DOGBERRY	If you meet a thief, you may suspect him, by virtue of your office, to be no true man; and for such kind of men, the less you meddle or make with them, why, the more is for your honesty. 41
2. WATCH	If we know him to be a thief, shall we not lay hands on him?
DOGBERRY	Truly, by your office you may; but I think they that touch pitch will be defil'd. The most peaceable way for you, if you do take a thief, is to let him show himself what he is, and steal out of your company. 46
VERGES	You have been always called a merciful man, partner.
DOGBERRY	Truly, I would not hang a dog by my will, much more a man who hath any honesty in him.
VERGES	If you hear a child cry in the night, you must call to the nurse and bid her still it. 51
2. WATCH	How if the nurse be asleep and will not hear us?
DOGBERRY	Why then, depart in peace and let the child wake her with crying; for the ewe that will not hear her lamb when it baes will never answer a calf when he bleats. 55
VERGES	'Tis very true.
DOGBERRY	This is the end of the charge: you, constable, are to present the Prince's own person. If you meet the Prince in the night, you may stay him.
VERGES	Nay, by'r lady, that I think 'a cannot. 60

---

32 **bills:** halberds, pikes. 36–37. **they are not...for:** you are disappointed in them. **true:** honest. 40–41. **meddle or make:** have to do with. —**the more...honesty:** the better for your respectability. 43–44. **touch pitch...defil'd.** he that touches pith (or tar) is dirtied by it; one who lays hands on a theif may be guilty by association. 54–55. **never answer a calf.** Thus Dogberry—though without any such intention—calls the watchman a calf. 57. **present:** represent. 59. **stay him:** stop him. 60. **by'r Lady:** by our Lady—an oath by the Virgin Mary.

DOGBERRY	Five shillings to one on't with any man that knows the statutes, he may stay him! Marry, not without the Prince be willing; for indeed the watch ought to offend no man, and it is an offence to stay a man against his will.
VERGES	By'r lady, I think it be so. 65
DOGBERRY	Ha, ah, ha! Well, masters, good night. An there be any matter of weight chances, call up me. Keep your fellows' counsels and your own, and good night. Come, neighbor.
2. WATCH	Well, masters, we hear our charge. Let us go sit here upon the church bench till two, and then all to bed. 70
DOGBERRY	One word more, honest neighbors. I pray you watch about Signior Leonato's door; for the wedding being there tomorrow, there is a great coil tonight. Adieu. Be vigitant, I beseech you.

Exeunt [Dogberry and Verges].

Enter Borachio and Conrade.

BORACHIO	What, Conrade!
2. WATCH	[*aside*] Peace! stir not! 75
BORACHIO	Conrade, I say!
CONRADE	Here, man. I am at thy elbow.
BORACHIO	Mass, and my elbow itch'd! I thought there would a scab follow.
CONRADE	I will owe thee an answer for that; and now forward with thy tale.
BORACHIO	Stand thee close then under this penthouse, for it drizzles rain, and I will, like a true drunkard, utter all to thee. 81
2. WATCH	[*aside*] Some treason, masters. Yet stand close.
BORACHIO	Therefore know I have earned of Don John a thousand ducats.
CONRADE	Is it possible that any villainy should be so dear?

---

61. **statutes:** The Quarto reading. The First Folio has "Statues," which some editors adopt for the sake of giving Dogberry one more blunder. 62. **Marry:** to be sure. 66. **Ha, ah, ha!** Dogberry clears his throat for a final instruction; but he cannot part without "one word more." 67. **counsels:** secrets. 69–70. **sit here upon the church bench:** take a nap on this bench in the porch outside the church. **coil:** hubbub. 73. **vigitant:** a blunder for *vigilant*. 78. **Mass.** A mere interjection; originally an oath by the mass. 78. **my elbow itch'd.** A traditional sign that somebody would soon be "at his elbow." —**scab.** With a pun on *scab* in the sense of "a scurvy fellow," "a worthless rogue." 79. **I will owe thee an answer for that:** I won't answer that insult now, but I shall not forget that I owe you a smart reply. 80. **under this penthouse:** A penthouse was a "lean-to"—an open shed having a roof with a single slope. 81. **like a true drunkard:** a genuine drunkard, who cannot hold his tongue—for "in vino veritas." The name *Borachio* means "drunkard" (Spanish *borracho*, "drunk," "drunkard"); but Borachio, though he has of course been drinking, is by no means drunk. 84. **dear:** costly.

BORACHIO	Thou shouldst rather ask if it were possible any villainy should 85 be so rich; for when rich villains have need of poor ones, poor ones may make what price they will.
CONRAD	I wonder at it.
BORACHIO	That shows thou art unconfirm'd. Thou knowest that the fashion of a doublet, or a hat, or a cloak, is nothing to a man. 90
CONRAD	Yes, it is apparel.
BORACHIO	I mean the fashion.
CONRAD	Yes, the fashion is the fashion.
BORACHIO	Tush! I may as well say the fool's the fool. But seest thou not what a deformed thief this fashion is? 95
2. WATCH	[aside] I know that Deformed. 'A has been a vile thief this seven year; 'a goes up and down like a gentleman. I remember his name.
BORACHIO	Didst thou not hear somebody?
CONRAD	No; 'twas the vane on the house. 99
BORACHIO	Seest thou not, I say, what a deformed thief this fashion is? how giddily 'a turns about all the hot-bloods between fourteen and five-and-thirty? sometimes fashioning them like Pharaoh's soldiers in the reechy painting, sometime like god Bel's priests in the old church window, sometime like the shaven Hercules in the smirch'd worm-eaten tapestry, where his codpiece seems as massy as his club? 106
CONRAD	All this I see; and I see that the fashion wears out more apparel than the man. But art not thou thyself giddy with the fashion too, that thou hast shifted out of thy tale into telling me of the fashion?

85–86. **any villainy should be so rich.** Borachio echoes Conrade's word *villainy* and personifies it: "The wonder is rather that villainy can afford to pay so high a price to get itself perpetrated." 89. **art unconfirm'd:** lack experience in villainy; are still a novice in that profession. 89–90. **the fashion... is nothing to a man:** The fashion is nothing in comparison with a man. This is the text of Borachio's sermon: "Fashions are always changing —they have no constancy. But men are even less constant than the fashion." He is leading up to his statement that Claudio has been suddenly transformed from Hero's lover to her bitter enemy. Conrade has no idea what Borachio is driving at; for he seems to him to be flying off at a tangent —changing the subject abruptly from "villainy" to "fashion." 95. **what a deformed thief:** what a contorted, shapeless rascal —having no constant or symmetrical figure; "and so," Borachio continues, "he sees to it that those who follow him have likewise no constancy." 97. **goes up and down like a gentleman:** walks about in gentleman's attire. 103. **reechy:** smoky. **—Bel's priests:** the priests of Baal in the legend of Bel and the Dragon in the biblical Apocrypha. 104. **the shaven Hercules.** This must have been an eccentric representation of a scene from the romantic episode of Hercules and Omphale. At all events it does not accord with any known version of the tale. 105. **codpiece.** A part of the breeches. 108. **giddy with the fashion:** just as changeable as the fashion is.

BORACHIO	Not so neither. But know that I have tonight wooed Margaret, the Lady Hero's gentlewoman, by the name of Hero. She leans me out at her mistress' chamber window, bids me a thousand times good night—I tell this tale vilely; I should first tell thee how the Prince, Claudio, and my master, planted and placed and possessed by my master Don John, saw afar off in the orchard this amiable encounter. 116
CONRAD	And thought they Margaret was Hero?
BORACHIO	Two of them did, the Prince and Claudio; but the devil my master knew she was Margaret; and partly by his oaths, which first possess'd them, partly by the dark night, which did deceive 120 them, but chiefly by my villainy, which did confirm any slander that Don John had made, away went Claudio enrag'd; swore he would meet her, as he was appointed, next morning at the temple, and there, before the whole congregation, shame her with what he saw o'ernight and send her home again without a husband. 125
2. WATCH	We charge you in the Prince's name stand!
1. WATCH	Call up the right Master Constable. We have here recover'd the most dangerous piece of lechery that ever was known in the commonwealth.
2. WATCH	And one Deformed is one of them. 130 I know him; 'a wears a lock.
CONRAD	Masters, masters—
1. WATCH	You'll be made bring Deformed forth, I warrant you.
CONRAD	Masters—
2. WATCH	Never speak, we charge you. Let us obey you to go with us. 135
BORACHIO	We are like to prove a goodly commodity, being taken up of these men's bills.
CONRAD	A commodity in question, I warrant you. Come, we'll obey you.

Exeunt.

---

110. **Not so neither:** Not a bit of it! I am sticking to the point. 114. **possessed:** taken possession of—as if Don John were a demon who had got them completely under his control. 115–16. **this amiable encounter:** this lovers' meeting. 120. **possess'd:** took possession of—and so, made them ready to believe anything. 127. **recover'd:** discovered. 128. **lechery:** for "villainy." 131. **a lock:** a long hanging lock of hair. Such locks were worn by fine gentlemen and sometimes also by ruffians. 135. **obey.** The Watchman means "induce." He is doing his best to follow Dogberry's principle: "The watch ought to offend no man." 136. **commodity:** lot of merchandise. **—taken up of these men's bills.** A pun: (1) "bought on credit by these men, who have given their bonds in payment"; (2) "arrested by these men's halberds."

SCENE IV. [*A room in Leonato's house.*]

Enter Hero, and Margaret and Ursula.

HERO   Good Ursula, wake my cousin Beatrice and desire her to rise.

URSULA   I will, lady.

HERO   And bid her come hither.

URSULA   Well.   [*Exit.*]

MARGARET   Troth, I think your other rebato were better.   5

HERO   No, pray thee, good Meg, I'll wear this.

MARGARET   By my troth 's not so good, and I warrant your cousin will say so.

HERO   My cousin's a fool, and thou art another. I'll wear none but this.

MARGARET   I like the new tire within excellently, if the hair were a thought
            browner; and your gown's a most rare fashion, i' faith. I saw the 10
            Duchess of Milan's gown that they praise so.

HERO   O, that exceeds, they say.

MARGARET   By my troth, 's but a nightgown in respect of yours—cloth-o'-gold
            and cuts, and lac'd with silver, set with pearls down sleeves, side-
            sleeves, and skirts, round underborne with a bluish tinsel. But   15
            for a fine, quaint, graceful, and excellent fashion, yours is worth
            ten on't.

HERO   God give me joy to wear it! for my heart is exceeding heavy.

MARGARET   'Twill be heavier soon by the weight of a man.

HERO   Fie upon thee! art not ashamed?   20

MARGARET   Of what, lady? of speaking honorably? Is not marriage honorable
            in a beggar? Is not your lord honorable without marriage? I think
            you would have me say, "saving your reverence, a husband." An bad

---

SCENE IV.
5. **rebato:** a stiff collar, supporting a ruff. **tire:** headdress. 9. **within:** i.e., the one which is in the inner
room. —**hair:** i.e., in the headdress. 12. **exceeds:** is superexcellent. 13. **nightgown:** dressing gown.
—**in respect of:** in comparison with. —**cloth-o'-gold:** cloth with gold threads woven in. 14. **cuts:**
slashes or openings in the skirt, which were either trimmed elaborately or filled in with a different
material. —**down:** down along. —**side-sleeves.** Besides the real sleeves (for the arms) there was a pair of
wide, open-hanging sleeves—merely for ornament. 15. **round underborne:** trimmed round the under
edge of the skirt. 16. **quaint:** elegant. 22. **in a beggar:** even in a beggar. 23. **saving your reverence.**
An apologetic phrase (*salva reverentia, save reverence*), "respect for you being preserved," i.e., "spoken
with no intention of offending you." This formula was often used in mentioning something indecent
or unpleasant, to assure the person addressed that no disrespect was intended. Margaret means that
Hero is so prudish that even the word *husband* cannot be mentioned without an apology for freedom
of speech.

thinking do not wrest true speaking, I'll offend nobody. Is there any harm in "the heavier for a husband"? None, I think, an it be the right husband and the right wife. Otherwise 'tis light, and not heavy. Ask my Lady Beatrice else. Here she comes.   27

Enter Beatrice.

HERO	Good morrow, coz.
BEATRICE	Good morrow, sweet Hero.
HERO	Why, how now? Do you speak in the sick tune? 30
BEATRICE	I am out of all other tune, methinks.
MARGARET	Clap's into "Light o' love." That goes without a burden. Do you sing it, and I'll dance it.
BEATRICE	Yea, "Light o' love" with your heels! then, if your husband have stables enough, you'll see he shall lack no barnes. 35
MARGARET	O illegitimate construction! I scorn that with my heels.
BEATRICE	'Tis almost five o'clock, cousin; 'tis time you were ready. By my troth, I am exceeding ill. Hey-ho!
MARGARET	For a hawk, a horse, or a husband?
BEATRICE	For the letter that begins them all, H. 40
MARGARET	Well, an you be not turn'd Turk, there's no more sailing by the star.
BEATRICE	What means the fool, trow?
MARGARET	Nothing I; but God send every one their heart's desire!
HERO	These gloves the Count sent me, they are an excellent perfume. 45

23–24. **An bad thinking...true speaking:** unless impure thoughts in the hearer's mind twist the sense of what is innocently meant by the speaker. 26. **light:** licentious—with a customary pun. 27. **Ask... else:** Ask my Lady Beatrice if what I say is not true, for she is a good judge of tricks of speech. 28. **Good morrow:** good morning. —**coz:** cousin. 30. **the sick tune?** Beatrice has answered in a melancholy tone, for she has a presentiment of ill fortune. 32. **Clap's into "Light o' love":** Change your tune immediately into the joy of loving. Probably there is a pun on *light* in the sense of "inconstant." The tune of the song has come down to us, but the words are lost. —**burden:** refrain. The *burden* of a song was the *base, foot,* or *under-song.* It was sung throughout, and not merely at the end of the verse. Beatrice puns on the word: "There's nothing heavy (sorrowful) about that song or that kind of love." 34. **Yea... heels!** Yes indeed! you say you'll dance it. If so, you'll be a light-stepper in love, easily led astray. 35. **barnes:** bairns, children—with an obvious pun. 36. **construction:** interpretation. —**I scorn that with my heels.** An old phrase for rejecting anything with contempt—kicking it away, like a horse. 40. **H:** an ache (pronounced *aitch*). 41–42. **Well...star.** Margaret implies that Beatrice's illness is an aching heart: "Well, if you haven't been false to your faith (renounced your vow never to marry), there's no trusting to the plainest signs —we can no longer put faith in the North Star as an indication of the points of the compass when we sail the seas." 43. **What...trow?** What do you suppose the fool means? *Trow* seems to be a clipped form of *trow ye* ("do you think?"), but is used as a mere interrogative particle, much like *pray.* 45. **perfume.** Perfumed gloves were fashionable in old times.

BEATRICE	I am stuff'd, cousin; I cannot smell.
MARGARET	A maid, and stuff'd! There's goodly catching of cold.
BEATRICE	O, God help me! God help me! How long have you profess'd apprehension?
MARGARET	Ever since you left it. Doth not my wit become me rarely? 50
BEATRICE	It is not seen enough. You should wear it in your cap. By my troth, I am sick.
MARGARET	Get you some of this distill'd carduus benedictus and lay it to your heart. It is the only thing for a qualm.
HERO	There thou prick'st her with a thistle. 55
BEATRICE	Benedictus? why benedictus? You have some moral in this "benedictus."
MARGARET	Moral? No, by my troth, I have no moral meaning; I meant plain holy thistle. You may think perchance that I think you are in love. Nay, by'r lady, I am not such a fool to think what I list; nor I 60 list not to think what I can; nor indeed I cannot think, if I would think my heart out of thinking, that you are in love, or that you will be in love, or that you can be in love. Yet Benedick was such another, and now is he become a man. He swore he would never marry; and yet now in despite of his heart he eats his meat 65 without grudging; and how you may be converted I know not, but methinks you look with your eyes as other women do.
BEATRICE	What pace is this that thy tongue keeps?
MARGARET	Not a false gallop.

Enter Ursula.

---

46. **I am stuff'd:** I have a cold in my head. Beatrice is accounting for her pretended illness. 47. **A maid, and stuffed!:** a bawdy pun by Margaret. 49. **apprehension:** quickness of wit. 51. **in your cap:** like a feather. 53. **this...carduus benedictus.** *This* is used in the colloquial sense (still common) to designate something that is much talked about. *Carduus benedictus* was an herb that was believed to have many health benefits [P.K.]. 54. **the only thing for a qualm:** the very best remedy for an attack of faintness. 56. **some moral:** some figurative meaning (like the "moral" of a fable). 60. **to think what I list:** as to think what I should like to think. 60–61. **nor...can:** nor am I pleased with the only thought that it is possible for me to have—namely, that you are not in love. —**nor...I cannot:** nor can I. —**if I would... thinking:** even if I should think so hard as to wear my heart out with the exertion and thus put an end to my thinking powers forever. 63. **will be:** will consent to be. —**can be:** i.e., even if you wished to be. 63–64. **such another:** another who was just like you—incapable of loving. —**a man:** a human being—with the natural instincts of humanity. 65–66. **in despite...he eats...grudging:** in spite of his most earnest resolution, he eats without objection the normal food of a human being—i.e., he is in love, as it is natural and proper that a man should be. —**how...know not:** to what extent you also have been brought into accord with human nature. 67. **as other women do:** and not as an unnatural opponent to love. 69. **a false gallop.** This means, literally, "a canter" (regarded as an artificial gait for a horse); but Margaret's meaning is clear: "Whatever you may say of the way in which my tongue runs, you cannot deny that it tells the truth—you *are* in love."

URSULA	Madam, withdraw. The Prince, the Count, Signior Benedick, 70 Don John, and all the gallants of the town are come to fetch you to church.
HERO	Help to dress me, good coz, good Meg, good Ursula. [*Exeunt.*]

SCENE V. [*The hall in Leonato's house.*]

Enter Leonato and the Constable [Dogberry] and the Headborough [Verges].

LEONATO	What would you with me, honest neighbor?
DOGBERRY	Marry, sir, I would have some confidence with you that decerns you nearly.
LEONATO	Brief, I pray you; for you see it is a busy time with me.
DOGBERRY	Marry, this it is, sir. 5
VERGES	Yes, in truth it is, sir.
LEONATO	What is it, my good friends?
DOGBERRY	Goodman Verges, sir, speaks a little off the matter—an old man, sir, and his wits are not so blunt as, God help, I would desire they were; but, in faith, honest as the skin between his brows. 10
VERGES	Yes, I thank God I am as honest as any man living that is an old man and no honester than I.
DOGBERRY	Comparisons are odorous. Palabras, neighbor Verges.
LEONATO	Neighbors, you are tedious.
DOGBERRY	It pleases your worship to say so, but we are the poor Duke's 15 officers; but truly, for mine own part, if I were as tedious as a king, I could find in my heart to bestow it all of your worship.
LEONATO	All thy tediousness on me, ah?

SCENE V.

Stage Direction **Headborough:** a local constable. 2. **confidence** sometimes means "private conversation;" but here it is merely Dogberry's blunder for "conference." —**decerns:** concerns. 8. **Goodman.** The regular title for one just below the rank of gentleman. —**a little off the matter:** not quite to the point. 9. **blunt:** for "sharp." Dogberry persists in saying the exact opposite of what he means. —**God help:** God help us all to keep our wits sound when we grow old! 10. **honest as...brows.** A proverbial comparison: "He has an honest forehead, and his heart is just as honest as his face." 11. **Yes, I thank God,** etc. Verges wishes to express himself modestly, with the air of one who declines to accept the full measure of a compliment. 13. **comparisons are odorous.** A distortion of the old saying "Comparisons are odious." —**palabras:** for the Spanish "pocas palabras," i.e., "few words," "don't talk too much." 15. **It pleases your worship to say so:** Your honor is so kind as to call us tedious; but, in fact, we are merely humble officers in the Duke's service. Dogberry takes *tedious* in the sense of "rich" or "prosperous," as if Leonato were paying him a compliment. 17. **it all:** all my "tediousness"—all the wealth I have. —**of:** on.

DOGBERRY	Yea, an 'twere a thousand pound more than 'tis; for I hear as good exclamation on your worship as of any man in the city; and though I be but a poor man, I am glad to hear it. 20
VERGES	And so am I.
LEONATO	I would fain know what you have to say.
VERGES	Marry, sir, our watch tonight, excepting your worship's presence, ha' ta'en a couple of as arrant knaves as any in Messina. 25
DOGBERRY	A good old man, sir; he will be talking. As they say, "When the age is in, the wit is out." God help us! it is a world to see! Well said, i' faith, neighbor Verges. Well, God's a good man. An two men ride of a horse, one must ride behind. An honest soul, i' faith, sir, by my troth he is, as ever broke bread; but God is to be worshipp'd; 30 all men are not alike, alas, good neighbor!
LEONATO	Indeed, neighbor, he comes too short of you.
DOGBERRY	Gifts that God gives.
LEONATO	I must leave you.
DOGBERRY	One word, sir. Our watch, sir, have indeed comprehended two 35 auspicious persons, and we would have them this morning examined before your worship.
LEONATO	Take their examination yourself and bring it me. I am now in great haste, as it may appear unto you.
DOGBERRY	It shall be suffigance. 40
LEONATO	Drink some wine ere you go. Fare you well.

[Enter a Messenger.]

MESSENGER	My lord, they stay for you to give your daughter to her husband.
LEONATO	I'll wait upon them. I am ready.

[Exeunt Leonato and Messenger.]

DOGBERRY	Go, good partner, go get you to Francis Seacoal; bid him bring

19–20. **as good an exclamation on:** as good acclamation of; as good report concerning. 24. **excepting...presence.** A perverted apologetic formula. Dogberry means: "if your honor will pardon me for using such words in speaking to you." His words, however, mean, literally, that the knaves who have been arrested are the greatest rascals in Messina "except your honorable self." 26–27. **When... out.** Dogberry's perversion of the old saying "When the wine is in, the wit is out." —**it is a world to see!** What a strange world we live in! This seems to be Dogberry's meaning; but the phrase usually means "It is a wonderful thing (one of the wonders of the world) to behold." 28. **God's a good man.** A quaint old phrase for "God is good." 29. **of a horse:** on one horse. —**one must ride behind.** Dogberry implies that it is the natural order of things for Verges to be his inferior in wisdom. 33. **Gifts that God gives.** Thus Dogberry piously ascribes his superiority to the grace of God—not to any merit of his own. 35. **comprehended:** for "apprehended," "arrested." 36. **auspicious:** for "suspicious." 40. **suffigance:** sufficiency—i.e., what you say shall suffice; we will follow your orders.

his pen and inkhorn to the jail. We are now to examination   45
these men.

VERGES   And we must do it wisely.

DOGBERRY   We will spare for no wit, I warrant you. Here's that shall drive
some of them to a noncome. Only get the learned writer to set
down our excommunication, and meet me at the jail. *Exeunt.*   50

ACT IV

SCENE I. [*A church.*]

Enter Don Pedro, [John the] Bastard, Leonato, Friar [Francis],
Claudio, Benedick, Hero, Beatrice, [and Attendants].

LEONATO   Come, Friar Francis, be brief. Only to the plain form of marriage,
and you shall recount their particular duties afterwards.

FRIAR   You come hither, my lord, to marry this lady?

CLAUDIO   No.

LEONATO   To be married to her. Friar, you come to marry her.   5

FRIAR   Lady, you come hither to be married to this count?

HERO   I do.

FRIAR   If either of you know any inward impediment why you should not
be conjoined, I charge you on your souls to utter it.

CLAUDIO   Know you any, Hero?   10

HERO   None, my lord.

FRIAR   Know you any, Count?

LEONATO   I dare make his answer—none.

CLAUDIO   O, what men dare do! what men may do! what men daily do, not

---

48. **We will spare for no wit:** We will not fail to use wisdom in our examination of them. —**Here's
that:** Here (in this head of mine) is that which, etc. 49. **a noncome:** a *non compos mentis.* This phrase,
which signifies "not of sound mind," is understood by Dogberry to mean "a non-plus," i.e., a condition
in which one does not know what to say or to do. 50. **our excommunication:** the details of our
examination of them. Dogberry regards this word as more emphatic than *examination.*
ACT IV. SCENE I.
1. **Only to the plain form:** Proceed only as far as the simple formula of the marriage ceremony prescribes.
2. **their particular duties.** It was the custom for the priest or clergyman to preface the marriage
ceremony with a brief sermon on the duties of husband and wife. 8–9. **know…utter it.** The Friar
follows the English marriage service, but not quite word for word. —**inward:** secret, undisclosed.

	knowing what they do!	15
BENEDICK	How now? interjections? Why then, some be of laughing, as, ah, ha, he!	
CLAUDIO	Stand thee by, friar. Father, by your leave: Will you with free and unconstrained soul Give me this maid your daughter?	20
LEONATO	As freely, son, as God did give her me.	
CLAUDIO	And what have I to give you back whose worth May counterpoise this rich and precious gift?	
DON PEDRO	Nothing, unless you render her again.	
CLAUDIO	Sweet Prince, you learn me noble thankfulness. There, Leonato, take her back again. Give not this rotten orange to your friend.† She's but the sign and semblance of her honor. Behold how like a maid she blushes here! O, what authority and show of truth Can cunning sin cover itself withal! Comes not that blood as modest evidence To witness simple virtue? Would you not swear, All you that see her, that she were a maid By these exterior shows? But she is none: She knows the heat of a luxurious bed; Her blush is guiltiness, not modesty.	25 30 35
LEONATO	What do you mean, my lord?	
CLAUDIO	Not to be married, Not to knit my soul to an approved wanton.	
LEONATO	Dear my lord, if you, in your own proof, Have vanquish'd the resistance of her youth And made defeat of her virginity—	40
CLAUDIO	I know what you would say. If I have known her,	

---

23. **May counterpoise:** can counterbalance. 25. **Sweet.** Common as a mere synonym for *dear.* —**learn:** teach. 30. **what authority...truth:** what assurance and what outward semblance of truth. 31. **withal:** with. Often so used at the end of a clause or sentence. 33. **simple:** pure and simple. 36. **luxurious:** lascivious; lewd [P.K.]. 39. **approved:** proved. 40. **your own proof:** your own experience.

---

†   In the BBC version, which is staged in a somber, shadowy chapel, Claudio steps upon the altar dais as he makes his accusations; he is joined by Don Pedro and Don John, who echo his claims, all emphasizing how their honor has been compromised by Hero's betrayal. Thus the men come together at the altar at the expense of the bride. [P. K.]

You will say she did embrace me as a husband,
And so extenuate the forehand sin.   45
No, Leonato,
I never tempted her with word too large,
But, as a brother to his sister, show'd
Bashful sincerity and comely love.

HERO   And seem'd I ever otherwise to you?   50

CLAUDIO   Out on the seeming! I will write against it.
You seem to me as Dian in her orb,
As chaste as is the bud ere it be blown;
But you are more intemperate in your blood
Than Venus, or those pamp'red animals   55
That rage in savage sensuality.

HERO   Is my lord well that he doth speak so wide?

LEONATO   Sweet Prince, why speak not you?

DON PEDRO   What should I speak?
I stand dishonor'd that have gone about
To link my dear friend to a common stale.   60

LEONATO   Are these things spoken, or do I but dream?

DON JOHN   Sir, they are spoken, and these things are true.

BENEDICK   This looks not like a nuptial.

HERO   "True!" O God!

CLAUDIO   Leonato, stand I here?
Is this the Prince? Is this the Prince's brother?   65
Is this face Hero's? Are our eyes our own?

LEONATO   All this is so; but what of this, my lord?

CLAUDIO   Let me but move one question to your daughter,
And by that fatherly and kindly power
That you have in her, bid her answer truly.   70

LEONATO   I charge thee do so, as thou art my child.

HERO   O, God defend me! How am I beset!

---

45. **the forehand sin:** the sinfulness of doing something before the proper time. 47. **large:** broad, free, immodest. 49. **comely:** becoming. 51. **Out on the seeming! I will write against it.** Shame upon such hypocrisy! I will write satires to denounce it. 52. **Dian:** Diana, the maiden goddess. —**orb:** sphere. Diana is also goddess of the moon. 53. **blown:** in blossom. **intemperate:** ungoverned. 57. **speak so wide:** talk so wildly—so far from the obvious facts. 59. **gone about:** undertaken, planned. 60. **stale:** harlot. 68. **move:** propose, put. 69. **that fatherly and kindly power:** that natural authority that you have as her father.

	What kind of catechising call you this?	
CLAUDIO	To make you answer truly to your name.	
HERO	Is it not Hero? Who can blot that name With any just reproach?	75
CLAUDIO	Marry, that can Hero! Hero itself can blot out Hero's virtue. What man was he talk'd with you yesternight, Out at your window betwixt twelve and one? Now, if you are a maid, answer to this.	80
HERO	I talk'd with no man at that hour, my lord.	
DON PEDRO	Why, then are you no maiden. Leonato, I am sorry you must hear. Upon mine honor, Myself, my brother, and this grieved Count Did see her, hear her, at that hour last night Talk with a ruffian at her chamber window, Who hath indeed, most like a liberal villain, Confess'd the vile encounters they have had A thousand times in secret.	85
JOHN	Fie, fie! they are not to be nam'd, my lord— Not to be spoke of; There is not chastity enough in language Without offence to utter them. Thus, pretty lady, I am sorry for thy much misgovernment.	90
CLAUDIO	O Hero! what a Hero hadst thou been If half thy outward graces had been plac'd About thy thoughts and counsels of thy heart! But fare thee well, most foul, most fair! Farewell, Thou pure impiety and impious purity! For thee I'll lock up all the gates of love, And on my eyelids shall conjecture hang, To turn all beauty into thoughts of harm, And never shall it more be gracious.	95 100

---

74. **answer truly to your name:** admit that the name by which you have been called is really yours. The name is "common stale" (i.e., whore). Hero does not understand the question. 76. **Marry, that can Hero!** Why, Hero herself can do so. 77. **Hero itself:** the very word Hero has become a name for a harlot. 80. **if you are a maid, answer to this:** If you are a maid, you can answer this question in such a way as will prove your innocence. 82. **then are you no maiden:** Your reply proves that you cannot answer that question truthfully without admitting your guilt. 84. **grieved:** aggrieved, wronged. 87. **liberal:** licentious in speech as in actions. 94. **much misgovernment:** great misconduct. 97. **thoughts and counsels:** secret thoughts. 100. **For thee:** because of thee and thy guilt. 101. **conjecture:** suspicion. 102. **thoughts of harm:** harmful (condemnatory) thoughts. 103. **never shall it more be gracious:** nevermore shall beauty seem beautiful to me.

Claudio accuses Hero of infidelity at their wedding ceremony. (Branagh, 1993)

LEONATO	Hath no man's dagger here a point for me? *[Hero swoons.]*	
BEATRICE	Why, how now, cousin? Wherefore sink you down?	105
DON JOHN	Come let us go. These things, come thus to light, Smother her spirits up. *[Exeunt Don Pedro, Don Juan, and Claudio.]†*	
BENEDICK	How doth the lady?	
BEATRICE	Dead, I think. Help, uncle! Hero! why, Hero! Uncle! Signior Benedick! Friar!	
LEONATO	O Fate, take not away thy heavy hand! Death is the fairest cover for her shame That may be wish'd for.	110
BEATRICE	How now, cousin Hero?	
FRIAR	Have comfort, lady.	
LEONATO	Dost thou look up?	
FRIAR	Yea, wherefore should she not?	
LEONATO	Wherefore? Why, doth not every earthly thing Cry shame upon her? Could she here deny	115

---

107. **her spirits:** her vital forces.

---

†   In Branagh's *Much Ado*, the soldiers are all attired in identical military uniforms, indicating their solidarity. After Claudio exposes Hero's "infidelity," they all, with the exception of Benedick, storm out together, knocking over chairs and tearing down wedding banners.

The story that is printed in her blood?
Do not live, Hero; do not ope thine eyes;
For, did I think thou wouldst not quickly die,
Thought I thy spirits were stronger than thy shames,   120
Myself would on the rearward of reproaches
Strike at thy life. Griev'd I, I had but one?
Chid I for that at frugal nature's frame?
O, one too much by thee! Why had I one?
Why ever wast thou lovely in my eyes?   125
Why had I not with charitable hand
Took up a beggar's issue at my gates,
Who smirched thus and mir'd with infamy,
I might have said, 'No part of it is mine;
This shame derives itself from unknown loins'?   130
But mine, and mine I lov'd, and mine I prais'd,
And mine that I was proud on—mine so much
That I myself was to myself not mine,
Valuing of her—why, she, O, she is fall'n
Into a pit of ink, that the wide sea   135
Hath drops too few to wash her clean again,
And salt too little which may season give
To her foul tainted flesh!

BENEDICK   Sir, sir, be patient.
For my part, I am so attir'd in wonder,
I know not what to say.   140

BEATRICE   O, on my soul, my cousin is belied!

BENEDICK   Lady, were you her bedfellow last night?

BEATRICE   No, truly, not; although, until last night,
I have this twelvemonth been her bedfellow.

LEONATO   Confirm'd, confirm'd! O, that is stronger made   145
Which was before barr'd up with ribs of iron!
Would the two princes lie? and Claudio lie,
Who lov'd her so that, speaking of her foulness,
Wash'd it with tears? Hence from her! let her die.

---

117. **The story...in her blood:** the story whose truth her blushes made perfectly clear—as plain as print.
120. **thy shames:** thy feelings of shame. 121. **on the rearward of reproaches:** after upbraiding thee.
123. **frugal nature's frame:** the stinginess of Nature in granting me only one child [P.K.]. 133–34. **mine
so much...Valuing of her:** she who was so much my beloved that, in comparison, I hardly cared for
myself at all, since I valued her so highly. 137. **may season give:** can restore to soundness —literally,
can preserve from decay. 138. **patient:** calm, self-controlled. 141. **belied:** misrepresented or slandered.
149. **Wash'd:** he washed.

FRIAR	Hear me a little;	150
	For I have only been silent so long,	
	And given way unto this course of fortune,	
	By noting of the lady. I have mark'd	
	A thousand blushing apparitions	
	To start into her face, a thousand innocent shames	155
	In angel whiteness beat away those blushes,	
	And in her eye there hath appear'd a fire	
	To burn the errors that these princes hold	
	Against her maiden truth. Call me a fool;	
	Trust not my reading nor my observation,	160
	Which with experimental seal doth warrant	
	The tenor of my book; trust not my age,	
	My reverence, calling, nor divinity,	
	If this sweet lady lie not guiltless here	
	Under some biting error.	
LEONATO	Friar, it cannot be.	165
	Thou seest that all the grace that she hath left	
	Is that she will not add to her damnation	
	A sin of perjury: she not denies it.	
	Why seek'st thou then to cover with excuse	
	That which appears in proper nakedness?	170
FRIAR	Lady, what man is he you are accus'd of?	
HERO	They know that do accuse me; I know none.	
	If I know more of any man alive	
	Than that which maiden modesty doth warrant,	
	Let all my sins lack mercy! O my father,	175
	Prove you that any man with me convers'd	
	At hours unmeet, or that I yesternight	
	Maintain'd the change of words with any creature,	
	Refuse me, hate me, torture me to death!	
FRIAR	There is some strange misprision in the princes.	180

151–53. **I…lady:** The only reason why I have so long remained silent and allowed fortune thus to run its course, is because I have been observing the lady. 154. **apparitions.** Thus the Friar personifies Hero's blushes. 158. **To burn the errors:** as heretics, holding false opinions, are burned at the stake. A natural metaphor for an ecclesiastic to use. The idea was that the errors were to be purged away by fire. 160. **my reading:** my ability to read character. 160–62. **my observation…book:** my observation of life, which, by the seal of experience, confirms my interpretation of what I have read in her face. —**the tenor of my book.** my education. 163. **My reverence:** my sacred profession. —**calling:** my priestly office (which has given me skill in reading character as a father confessor). —**divinity:** my theological study and training. 165. **Under:** as the victim of. 166. **grace:** virtue. 170. **proper:** its own. 176. **Prove you:** if you can prove. 177. **unmeet:** improper, unbecoming. 178. **change:** exchange. 179. **Refuse me:** cast me off. 180. **misprision:** mistake.

BENEDICK   Two of them have the very bent of honor;
             And if their wisdoms be misled in this,
             The practice of it lives in John the bastard,
             Whose spirits toil in frame of villanies.

LEONATO   I know not. If they speak but truth of her,   185
             These hands shall tear her. If they wrong her honor,
             The proudest of them shall well hear of it.
             Time hath not yet so dried this blood of mine,
             Nor age so eat up my invention,
             Nor fortune made such havoc of my means,   190
             Nor my bad life reft me so much of friends,
             But they shall find awak'd in such a kind
             Both strength of limb and policy of mind,
             Ability in means, and choice of friends,
             To quit me of them thoroughly.

FRIAR   Pause awhile   195
             And let my counsel sway you in this case.
             Your daughter here the princes left for dead,
             Let her awhile be secretly kept in,
             And publish it that she is dead indeed;
             Maintain a mourning ostentation,   200
             And on your family's old monument
             Hang mournful epitaphs, and do all rites
             That appertain unto a burial.

LEONATO   What shall become of this? What will this do?

FRIAR   Marry, this well carried shall on her behalf   205
             Change slander to remorse. That is some good.
             But not for that dream I on this strange course,
             But on this travail look for greater birth.
             She dying, as it must be so maintain'd,

---

181. **have the very bent of honor:** are entirely devoted to honor in thought and action. 183. **practice:** plotting. —**lives in:** owes its life and strength to. 184. **Whose...villainies:** whose whole strength is used to the utmost to devise and carry out villainous plans. 189. **my invention:** my inventive powers; my power to make plans. 192. **in such a kind:** in such a manner; to such an extent. 193. **policy of mind:** mental power in planning. 194. **means:** wealth. 195. **To quit me of them thoroughly:** to enable me to settle accounts with them thoroughly. With the Friar's plan we may well compare the rôle of Friar Laurence in *Romeo and Juliet.* 198. **in:** at home. 200. **a mourning ostentation:** a formal show of mourning rites. *Ostentation* suggests such an elaborate ceremony as might be expected in a family of very high rank. 202. **Hang mournful epitaphs.** Such was the custom in Shakespeare's day. See 5.3. 204. **What shall become of this?** What is to be the outcome of all this course of action? 205. **well carried:** if well carried out, managed. —**shall:** will certainly. 206. **remorse:** compassion. 207. **on:** as the result of. 208. **travail.** This word, as here used, combines the meaning "toil," "effort," with that of "labor in childbirth." —**look for greater birth:** expect something more important than the mere change of slander to pity. 209. **as it must be so maintain'd:** as you must insist was the fact.

Upon the instant that she was accus'd,   210
Shall be lamented, pitied, and excus'd
Of every hearer; for it so falls out
That what we have we prize not to the worth
Whiles we enjoy it, but being lack'd and lost,
Why, then we rack the value, then we find   215
The virtue that possession would not show us
Whiles it was ours. So will it fare with Claudio.
When he shall hear she died upon his words,
Th' idea of her life shall sweetly creep
Into his study of imagination,   220
And every lovely organ of her life
Shall come apparell'd in more precious habit,
More moving, delicate, and full of life,
Into the eye and prospect of his soul
Than when she liv'd indeed. Then shall he mourn   225
(If ever love had interest in his liver)
And wish he had not so accused her—
No, though he thought his accusation true.
Let this be so, and doubt not but success
Will fashion the event in better shape   230
Than I can lay it down in likelihood.
But if all aim but this be levell'd false,
The supposition of the lady's death
Will quench the wonder of her infamy.
And if it sort not well, you may conceal her,   235
As best befits her wounded reputation,
In some reclusive and religious life,
Out of all eyes, tongues, minds, and injuries.

BENEDICK   Signior Leonato, let the friar advise you;
And though you know my inwardness and love   240

---

211. **Shall be:** will certainly be. 212. **Of:** by. 213. **to the worth:** to its full value. 214. **Whiles:** so long as. 215. **we rack the value:** we strain the valuation to the utmost limit. 216. **virtue:** excellence. 218. **upon:** because of; as the result of. 219. **Th' idea of her life:** the thought of her as she was when alive. 220. **Into his study of imagination:** into his imagination when he thinks of her. 221. **organ of her life:** of her as she was when alive. *Organ* includes all the bodily organs that give expression to one's personality —in eye, voice, motion, etc. 224. **the eye and prospect of his soul:** his soul's eye and imaginative sight. *Soul* is the emphatic word. 226. **had interest in:** could claim a share in. —**liver.** Thought in old times to be the seat of the passion of love. 229. **Let this be so:** Assume (as it is very likely) that what I have predicted comes true. —**success:** the sequel; time as it goes forward. 230. **the event:** the outcome. 232. **But...false:** But if all my forecast should turn out to be mistaken except *this* point, *this* at least will be accomplished—the belief that Hero has died will make people cease to dwell upon her shame. —**aim:** guess, conjecture, forecast. —**levell'd false:** aimed amiss. 235. **if it sort not well:** if my plan does not result successfully. 237. **reclusive:** cloistered—as the life of a nun. 238. **injuries:** insults. 239. **let the friar advise you:** take the friar's advice. 240. **inwardness and love:** intimate friendship.

Is very much unto the Prince and Claudio,
Yet, by mine honor, I will deal in this
As secretly and justly as your soul
Should with your body.

LEONATO   Being that I flow in grief,
The smallest twine may lead me.   245

FRIAR   'Tis well consented. Presently away;
For to strange sores strangely they strain the cure.
Come, lady, die to live. This wedding day
Perhaps is but prolong'd. Have patience and endure.
                    Exeunt [all but Benedick and Beatrice].

BENEDICK   Lady Beatrice, have you wept all this while?   250

BEATRICE   Yea, and I will weep a while longer.

BENEDICK   I will not desire that.

BEATRICE   You have no reason. I do it freely.

BENEDICK   Surely I do believe your fair cousin is wronged.   254

BEATRICE   Ah, how much might the man deserve of me that would right her!

BENEDICK   Is there any way to show such friendship?

BEATRICE   A very even way, but no such friend.

BENEDICK   May a man do it?

BEATRICE   It is a man's office, but not yours.   259

BENEDICK   I do love nothing in the world so well as you. Is not that strange?

BEATRICE   As strange as the thing I know not. It were as possible for me to
say I loved nothing so well as you. But believe me not; and yet I
lie not. I confess nothing, nor I deny nothing. I am sorry for my
cousin.

BENEDICK   By my sword, Beatrice, thou lovest me.   265

BEATRICE   Do not swear, and eat it.

---

244. **Should:** certainly would. —**Being that I flow in grief:** since I am dissolved in tears and therefore
have no strength left. 246. **'Tis well consented:** You do well in consenting to my proposal. —**Presently:**
without delay. 247. **to strange sores strangely they strain the cure.** *They* is used in the indefinite sense
(as in "they say"): "To heal strange sores people use heroic treatment." To *strain the cure* is, literally, to
"apply violent remedies." 249. **prolong'd:** merely put off (postponed) and not given up. 253. **freely:**
willingly—and therefore no request from you is needed. 257. **A very even way:** a very level road,
without obstacles; an easy way. 258. **May:** can. "Is it within human power?" 259. **It...yours:** Yes, it is a
service that a man can do, but *you* are not the man to do it. 261. **As strange...know not:** as much of a
stranger as something that I am unacquainted with. Beatrice plays with the word *strange.* 262. **I loved
nothing so well as you.** Intentionally ambiguous: (1) I loved you more than I love anything else; (2) I
loved you no better than I love nothing at all. 266. **Do not swear, and eat it:** i.e., eat the words of your
assertion—take back (retract) your assertion that you love me, for it is false. Benedick understands her
to mean "eat your sword," and that phrase was undoubtedly also in her mind.

BENEDICK	I will swear by it that you love me, and I will make him eat it that says I love not you.
BEATRICE	Will you not eat your word?
BENEDICK	With no sauce that can be devised to it. I protest I love thee. 270
BEATRICE	Why then, God forgive me!
BENEDICK	What offence, sweet Beatrice?
BEATRICE	You have stayed me in a happy hour. I was about to protest I loved you.
BENEDICK	And do it with all thy heart. 275
BEATRICE	I love you with so much of my heart that none is left to protest.
BENEDICK	Come, bid me do anything for thee.
BEATRICE	Kill Claudio.
BENEDICK	Ha! not for the wide world!
BEATRICE	You kill me to deny it. Farewell. 280
BENEDICK	Tarry, sweet Beatrice.
BEATRICE	I am gone, though I am here. There is no love in you. Nay, I pray you let me go.
BENEDICK	Beatrice—
BEATRICE	In faith, I will go. 285
BENEDICK	We'll be friends first.
BEATRICE	You dare easier be friends with me than fight with mine enemy.
BENEDICK	Is Claudio thine enemy?
BEATRICE	Is 'a not approved in the height a villain, that hath slandered, 289 scorned, dishonored my kinswoman? O that I were a man! What? bear her in hand until they come to take hands, and then with public accusation, uncover'd slander, unmitigated rancor—O God, that I were a man! I would eat his heart in the market place.
BENEDICK	Hear me, Beatrice!
BEATRICE	Talk with a man out at a window!—a proper saying! 295

267. **I will make him eat it:** i.e., eat my sword. To "make a man eat one's sword" was a grotesque idiom for to "force him to submit or be killed." 271. **God forgive me!** i.e., for being so bold as to declare my love. 273. **You have stayed me in a happy hour:** You have interrupted me at an opportune moment—for I was about to be so forward as to declare that *I* loved *you.* 280. **to deny it:** by refusing to kill him. 282. **I am gone:** I am gone from you; I give you up. —**though I am here:** though you are holding me here and will not let me depart. 289. **approved:** proved to be. 291. **bear her in hand:** delude her. The phrase implies not merely a single act but a systematic course of deception. 292. **uncover'd:** outspoken. 295. **a proper saying!** a fine thing to say! a likely story!

BENEDICK	Nay, but Beatrice—
BEATRICE	Sweet Hero! she is wrong'd, she is sland'red, she is undone.
BENEDICK	Beat—

BEATRICE   Princes and Counties! Surely a princely testimony, a goodly count, Count Comfect, a sweet gallant surely! O that I were a man   300 for his sake! or that I had any friend would be a man for my sake! But manhood is melted into curtsies, valor into compliment, and men are only turn'd into tongue, and trim ones too. He is now as valiant as Hercules that only tells a lie, and swears it. I cannot be a man with wishing; therefore I will die a woman with grieving. 305

BENEDICK	Tarry, good Beatrice. By this hand, I love thee.
BEATRICE	Use it for my love some other way than swearing by it.
BENEDICK	Think you in your soul the Count Claudio hath wrong'd Hero?
BEATRICE	Yea, as sure as I have a thought or a soul. 309

BENEDICK   Enough, I am engag'd, I will challenge him. I will kiss your hand, and so I leave you. By this hand, Claudio shall render me a dear account. As you hear of me, so think of me. Go comfort your cousin. I must say she is dead—and so farewell.   [*Exeunt.*]

SCENE II. [*A prison.*]

Enter the Constables [Dogberry and Verges] and the Sexton, in gowns, [and the Watch, with Conrade and] Borachio.

DOGBERRY	Is our whole dissembly appear'd?†
VERGES	O, a stool and a cushion for the sexton.
SEXTON	Which be the malefactors?

---

297. **undone:** ruined. 299. **Counties!** Counts! —**a goodly count.** A bitter pun: "A handsome count and a fine story." 300. **Comfect:** Comfit; Sweetmeat. 301. **for his sake:** i.e., that I might take vengeance on him. —**would be:** who would be. 302. **curtsies:** curtsies. 303. **only:.** The implication is that men dare not fight in support of what they say. —**trim ones too:** fine tongues; fine talkers. 310. **I am engag'd:** I pledge myself. 311–312. **Claudio shall render me a dear account:** I will call Claudio to account and make him pay dear for his offence.

SCENE II.
1. **dissembly.** For "assembly." 2. **a cushion.** Some critics think that the cushion was to serve as a lap-tablet since the Sexton (who is also Town Clerk) was to take notes of the examination. They call attention to the bust of Shakespeare in the church at Stratford, which shows a cushion used for such a purpose. But probably Verges merely wishes to accommodate the Town Clerk with a dignified and comfortable seat.

---

†   In Antoon's film, this scene takes place is a country courthouse. Behind the judge's bench hangs a portrait of Dogberry, which he replaces with a portrait of President Roosevelt before the Sexton enters. [P.K.]

DOGBERRY	Marry, that am I and my partner.	
VERGES	Nay, that's certain. We have the exhibition to examine.	5
SEXTON	But which are the offenders that are to be examined? let them come before Master Constable.	
DOGBERRY	Yea, marry, let them come before me. What is your name, friend?	
BORACHIO	Borachio.	10
DOGBERRY	Pray write down Borachio. Yours, sirrah?	
CONRADE	I am a gentleman, sir, and my name is Conrade.	
DOGBERRY	Write down Master Gentleman Conrade. Masters, do you serve God?	
BOTH	Yea, sir, we hope.	15
DOGBERRY	Write down that they hope they serve God; and write God first, for God defend but God should go before such villains! Masters, it is proved already that you are little better than false knaves, and it will go near to be thought so shortly. How answer you for yourselves?	20
CONRADE	Marry, sir, we say we are none.	
DOGBERRY	A marvellous witty fellow, I assure you; but I will go about with him. Come you hither, sirrah. A word in your ear. Sir, I say to you, it is thought you are false knaves.	
BORACHIO	Sir, I say to you we are none.	25
DOGBERRY	Well, stand aside. Fore God, they are both in a tale. Have you writ down that they are none?	
SEXTON	Master Constable, you go not the way to examine. You must call forth the watch that are their accusers.	
DOGBERRY	Yea, marry, that's the eftest way. Let the watch come forth. Masters, I charge you in the Prince's name accuse these men.	30
1. WATCH	This man said, sir, that Don John the Prince's brother was a villain.	

---

5. **the exhibition:** the commission. 11. **sirrah:** fellow. *Sirrah* is a form of *sir*, often used in addressing an inferior or to express contempt or anger. Conrade resents Dogberry's use of the term. 13. **Masters.** Regularly used in respectful address, like the modern "gentlemen." Perhaps Dogberry has been impressed by Conrade's dignified answer; but it is unsafe to interpret his mental and linguistic capers. 17. **defend:** forbid. 21. **we are none.** An emphatic denial: "we are nothing of the kind." **witty:** clever, sharp. 22–23. **go about with him:** manage him. 26. **they are both in a tale:** they both tell one and the same story. 30. **marry:** to be sure. —**eftest:** easiest, most convenient, quickest. The word is unknown elsewhere.

DOGBERRY	Write down Prince John a villain. Why, this is flat perjury, to call a prince's brother villain. 35
BORACHIO	Master Constable—
DOGBERRY	Pray thee, fellow, peace. I do not like thy look, I promise thee.
SEXTON	What heard you him say else?
2. WATCH	Marry, that he had received a thousand ducats of Don John for accusing the Lady Hero wrongfully. 40
DOGBERRY	Flat burglary as ever was committed.
VERGES	Yea, by th' mass, that it is.
SEXTON	What else, fellow?
1. WATCH	And that Count Claudio did mean, upon his words, to disgrace Hero before the whole assembly, and not marry her. 45
DOGBERRY	O villain! thou wilt be condemn'd into everlasting redemption for this.
SEXTON	What else?
WATCHMEN	This is all. 49
SEXTON	And this is more, masters, than you can deny. Prince John is this morning secretly stol'n away. Hero was in this manner accus'd, in this very manner refus'd, and upon the grief of this suddenly died. Master Constable, let these men be bound and brought to Leonato's. I will go before and show him their examination.[*Exit.*]
DOGBERRY	Come, let them be opinion'd. 55
VERGES	Let them be in the hands—
CONRADE	Off, coxcomb!
DOGBERRY	God's my life, where's the sexton? Let him write down the Prince's officer coxcomb. Come, bind them.—Thou naughty varlet!
CONRADE	Away! you are an ass, you are an ass. 60
DOGBERRY	Dost thou not suspect my place? Dost thou not suspect my years? O that he were here to write me down an ass! But, masters, remember that I am an ass. Though it be not written down, yet forget not

---

44. **upon his words:** because of Borachio's story. 46. **redemption:** for "damnation." 52. **refus'd:** cast off (by Claudio). 55. **opinion'd:** for "pinioned." To *pinion* a man is to tie his hands behind his back, or to tie his elbows together behind him. 57. **coxcomb:** fool. Jesters wore in the cap a piece of red flannel imitating the comb of a cock. 58. **God's my life.** A common exclamation: "God save my life!" used much like our "Bless my soul!" 59. **naughty:** wicked. A strong adjective in Shakespeare's time—not, as now-a-days, degraded to the language of the nursery or of mild humor. —**varlet:** fellow, scamp. 61. **suspect:** for "respect." 62. **he:** the Sexton, who has just gone out.

that I am an ass. No, thou villain, thou art full of piety, as shall be
prov'd upon thee by good witness. I am a wise fellow; and which is
more, an officer; and which is more, a householder; and which is
more, as pretty a piece of flesh as any is in Messina, and one that
knows the law, go to! and a rich fellow enough, go to! and a fellow
that hath had losses; and one that hath two gowns and everything
handsome about him. Bring him away. O that I had been writ
down an ass!   *Exeunt.* 71

ACT V

SCENE I. [*The street, near Leonato's house.*]

Enter Leonato and his brother [Antonio].

ANTONIO   If you go on thus, you will kill yourself,
              And 'tis not wisdom thus to second grief
              Against yourself.

LEONATO   I pray thee cease thy counsel,
              Which falls into mine ears as profitless
              As water in a sieve. Give not me counsel,   5
              Nor let no comforter delight mine ear
              But such a one whose wrongs do suit with mine.
              Bring me a father that so lov'd his child,
              Whose joy of her is overwhelm'd like mine,
              And bid him speak to me of patience.   10
              Measure his woe the length and breadth of mine,
              And let it answer every strain for strain,
              As thus for thus, and such a grief for such,
              In every lineament, branch, shape, and form.
              If such a one will smile and stroke his beard,   15
              Bid sorrow wag, cry "hem" when he should groan,

---

67. **as pretty...in Messina.** As handsome a man as any in Messina [P.K.] 69. **that hath had losses.** For a
man who is still well-to-do to speak of his losses with a degree of self-complacency is a rather customary
trick of human nature.
ACT V. SCENE I.
2. **to second grief:** to give way to grief and thus to aid and abet its effect upon you. 7. **whose...mine:**
whose misfortunes are comparable to mine. 9. **whose...mine:** and whose delight in having her for his
daughter has been so annihilated by losing her. 10. **patience:** self-control. 12. **let it answer every strain
for strain:** let his sorrow match my sorrow in every point—feature for feature, trait for trait. 15. **smile
and stroke his beard:** like an aged philosopher. 16. **wag:** be off; go its way. —**cry "hem":** calmly clear
his throat.

Patch grief with proverbs, make misfortune drunk
With candle-wasters—bring him yet to me,
And I of him will gather patience.
But there is no such man; for, brother, men   20
Can counsel and speak comfort to that grief
Which they themselves not feel; but, tasting it,
Their counsel turns to passion, which before
Would give preceptial medicine to rage,
Fetter strong madness in a silken thread,   25
Charm ache with air and agony with words.
No, no! 'Tis all men's office to speak patience
To those that wring under the load of sorrow,
But no man's virtue nor sufficiency
To be so moral when he shall endure   30
The like himself. Therefore give me no counsel.
My griefs cry louder than advertisement.

ANTONIO   Therein do men from children nothing differ.

LEONATO   I pray thee peace. I will be flesh and blood;
For there was never yet philosopher   35
That could endure the toothache patiently,
However they have writ the style of gods
And made a push at chance and sufferance.

ANTONIO   Yet bend not all the harm upon yourself.
Make those that do offend you suffer too.   40

LEONATO   There thou speak'st reason. Nay, I will do so.
My soul doth tell me Hero is belied;
And that shall Claudio know; so shall the Prince,
And all of them that thus dishonor her.

Enter Don Pedro and Claudio.

---

17. **Patch grief with proverbs:** mend his grief by reciting scraps of proverbial wisdom. Such "wise saws" exist in abundance: "What can't be cured must be endured"; "The darkest hour is before the dawn"; "When bale is highest, boot [i.e., amendment, help] is nighest"; "He that is down need fear no fall." 17–18. **make misfortune drunk With candle-wasters:** stupefy his sorrow by means of precepts derived from philosophers who spend the night hours in composing stoical treatises. —**yet.** Emphatic: "after all"; "even now, when I am overwhelmed with grief." 19. **of him:** from him. 22. **tasting it:** when they actually *feel* grief. 23. **turns to passion:** is transformed to passionate sorrow. 23–24. **which before... to rage:** which—before they felt any sorrow themselves—undertook to cure the intensity of others' grief by mere consolatory precepts. 27. **all men's office:** everybody's service; something anybody and everybody is ready and able to do. 28. **wring:** are writhing. 29. **But no man's virtue nor sufficiency... himself:** but no one has the strength or the ability to moralize in that fashion when he is doomed to suffer such sorrow himself. 32. **cry louder than advertisement:** are too intense to be pacified by mere advice. 37. **However:** no matter how godlike (and therefore superior to humanity) is the way in which they have expressed themselves in their writings. 38. **made a push at...sufferance:** met misfortune and suffering with defiant courage. A *push* is an "attack," an "onset." —**sufferance:** suffering. 39. **bend:** direct. —**upon:** against.

ANTONIO	Here comes the Prince and Claudio hastily.	45
DON PEDRO	Good den, good den.	
CLAUDIO	Good day to both of you.	
LEONATO	Hear you, my lords!	
DON PEDRO	We have some haste, Leonato.	
LEONATO	Some haste, my lord! well, fare you well, my lord. Are you so hasty now? Well, all is one.	
DON PEDRO	Nay, do not quarrel with us, good old man.	50
ANTONIO	If he could right himself with quarrelling, Some of us would lie low.	
CLAUDIO	Who wrongs him?	
LEONATO	Marry, thou dost wrong me, thou dissembler, thou! Nay, never lay thy hand upon thy sword; I fear thee not.	
CLAUDIO	Marry, beshrew my hand	55

CLAUDIO   If it should give your age such cause of fear.
In faith, my hand meant nothing to my sword.

LEONATO   Tush, tush, man! never fleer and jest at me.
I speak not like a dotard nor a fool,
As under privilege of age to brag   60
What I have done being young, or what would do,
Were I not old. Know, Claudio, to thy head,
Thou hast so wrong'd mine innocent child and me
That I am forc'd to lay my reverence by
And, with grey hairs and bruise of many days,   65
Do challenge thee to trial of a man.
I say thou hast belied mine innocent child;
Thy slander hath gone through and through her heart,
And she lies buried with her ancestors—
O, in a tomb where never scandal slept,   70
Save this of hers, fram'd by thy villainy!

---

45. **comes.** A singular verb with two subjects is especially common when the verb comes first. 46. **Good den:** good even, good afternoon. 49. **all is one:** no matter; it makes no difference. 51. **right himself:** restore himself to a condition of happiness. Claudio's question shows that he does not understand Antonio's meaning. 55. **beshrew:** a mild word for "curse." 57. **meant nothing to my sword.** Leonato's excitement had caused Claudio instinctively to lay his hand upon his sword. He now disclaims any hostile intention: "My hand conveyed no meaning to my sword—did not suggest to my sword that I intended to draw it." 58. **fleer:** jeer. 60. **As...brag:** as if I were using the privilege which old men enjoy. 62. **to thy head:** as a direct challenge to thee. 64. **to lay my reverence by:** to renounce the right which the customary respect for old age gives me—namely, the privilege of exemption from fighting duels. 66. **to trial of a man:** to a test of strength and valor.

CLAUDIO   My villainy?

LEONATO   Thine, Claudio; thine I say.

DON PEDRO   You say not right, old man.

LEONATO   My lord, my lord,
                 I'll prove it on his body if he dare,
                 Despite his nice fence and his active practice,   75
                 His May of youth and bloom of lustihood.

CLAUDIO   Away! I will not have to do with you.

LEONATO   Canst thou so daff me? Thou hast kill'd my child.
                 If thou kill'st me, boy, thou shalt kill a man.

ANTONIO   He shall kill two of us, and men indeed.   80
                 But that's no matter; let him kill one first.
                 Win me and wear me! Let him answer me.
                 Come, follow me, boy. Come, sir boy, come follow me.
                 Sir boy, I'll whip you from your foining fence!
                 Nay, as I am a gentleman, I will.   85

LEONATO   Brother—

ANTONIO   Content yourself. God knows I lov'd my niece,
                 And she is dead, slander'd to death by villains,
                 That dare as well answer a man indeed
                 As I dare take a serpent by the tongue.   90
                 Boys, apes, braggarts, Jacks, milksops!

LEONATO   Brother Anthony—

ANTONIO   Hold you content. What, man! I know them, yea,
                 And what they weigh, even to the utmost scruple,
                 Scambling, outfacing, fashion-monging boys,
                 That lie and cog and flout, deprave and slander,   95
                 Go anticly, show outward hideousness,
                 And speak off half a dozen dang'rous words,
                 How they might hurt their enemies, if they durst;
                 And this is all.

---

75. **his nice fence:** his dexterity in fencing. 76. **lustihood:** vigour. 78. **daff me?** put me aside? 82. **Win me and wear me!** "Win it and wear it" was a common phrase, used either to call a man to action or to intimate that he cannot get the desired object without a contest: "Win it and it shall be yours to enjoy." Antonio applies the saying as a challenge: "Overcome me, and I will submit to be your humble servant"; "Come on, and let the best man win!" —**answer me:** meet *me* in response to my challenge. *Me* is emphatic. 84. **I'll whip you from your foining fence!** I'll parry your fencing thrusts with a whip! That will be a sufficient weapon to use against a youngster like you. A *foin* is a "thrust." 87. **Content yourself:** Be quiet and let me alone. 89. **answer a man indeed:** stand their ground in opposition to a real man. 91. **Jacks:** good-for-nothing fellows. 94. **Scambling:** quarrelsome. —**outfacing:** impudent. 95. **cog:** cheat. —**flout:** jeer. 96. **Go anticly:** swagger in fantastic attire. 99. **this is all:** this is all there is to them; this is the whole story. [P.K.]

LEONATO	But, brother Anthony—
ANTONIO	Come, 'tis no matter. 100 Do not you meddle; let me deal in this.
DON PEDRO	Gentlemen both, we will not wake your patience. My heart is sorry for your daughter's death; But, on my honor, she was charg'd with nothing But what was true, and very full of proof. 105
LEONATO	My lord, my lord—
DON PEDRO	I will not hear you.
LEONATO	No? Come, brother, away!—I will be heard.
ANTONIO	And shall, or some of us will smart for it. *Exeunt ambo.*

Enter Benedick.

DON PEDRO	See, see! Here comes the man we went to seek. 110
CLAUDIO	Now, signior, what news?
BENEDICK	Good day, my lord.
DON PEDRO	Welcome, signior. You are almost come to part almost a fray.
CLAUDIO	We had lik'd to have had our two noses snapp'd off with two old men without teeth. 115
DON PEDRO	Leonato and his brother. What think'st thou? Had we fought, I doubt we should have been too young for them.
BENEDICK	In a false quarrel there is no true valor. I came to seek you both.
CLAUDIO	We have been up and down to seek thee; for we are high-proof melancholy, and would fain have it beaten away. Wilt thou use thy wit? 121
BENEDICK	It is in my scabbard. Shall I draw it?
DON PEDRO	Dost thou wear thy wit by thy side?
CLAUDIO	Never any did so, though very many have been beside their wit. I will bid thee draw, as we do the minstrels—draw to pleasure us.
DON PEDRO	As I am an honest man, he looks pale. 126 Art thou sick or angry?

---

100. **'tis no matter:** this is nothing that you need worry about. 101. **let me deal in this:** let me manage this affair. 102. **we will not wake your patience:** we do not wish to disturb your serenity, i.e., to irritate you. 109. **shall:** you shall be heard. **Exeunt ambo:** They depart together. 113. **You are...a fray:** You arrive just too late to keep the peace in what was almost a brawl. 114. **We had lik'd to have had:** We were likely to have; we seemed to be on the point of having. **—with:** by. 117. **I doubt:** I suspect; I rather think. 118. **a false quarrel:** a quarrel in which the right is not on one's side. 119. **high-proof:** proof in the highest degree. 120. **fain:** gladly. 121. **wit:** cleverness in talk. 124. **beside their wit:** out of their wits; out of their minds. 125. **draw.** Claudio puns on drawing one's wit (as if it were a sword) and drawing the bow (of a fiddle).

CLAUDIO	What, courage, man! What though care kill'd a cat, thou hast mettle enough in thee to kill care.
BENEDICK	Sir, I shall meet your wit in the career an you charge it against me. I pray you choose another subject. 131
CLAUDIO	Nay then, give him another staff; this last was broke cross.
DON PEDRO	By this light, he changes more and more. I think he be angry indeed.
CLAUDIO	If he be, he knows how to turn his girdle. 135
BENEDICK	Shall I speak a word in your ear?
CLAUDIO	God bless me from a challenge!
BENEDICK	[aside to Claudio] You are a villain. I jest not; I will make it good how you dare, with what you dare, and when you dare. Do me right, or I will protest your cowardice. You have kill'd a sweet lady, and her death shall fall heavy on you. Let me hear from you.† 141
CLAUDIO	Well, I will meet you, so I may have good cheer.
DON PEDRO	What, a feast? a feast?
CLAUDIO	I' faith, I thank him, he hath bid me to a calve's head and a capon, the which if I do not carve most curiously, say my knife's naught. Shall I not find a woodcock too? 146

---

128. **care kill'd a cat:** even a *cat*. Cats, since they have nine lives, are hard to kill. 129. **mettle:** vivacity: liveliness of mind. 130. **in the career:** at full speed. **—an you charge it against me:** if you come charging on with it in an attack on me. The figures come from single combat on horseback in battle or tournament. 132. **another staff.** Claudio continues the tournament metaphor. *Another staff* may mean "another shaft for his lance" or, perhaps, "another lance"; but probably Claudio implies that this contest of wit is merely a mock tournament, in which poles are used instead of pointed lances. **—this last was broke cross:** this last witticism of his was a complete failure. **—cross:** across, crosswise. 133. **By this light.** A trivial oath "by the light of day." 135. **to turn his girdle:** "If you are angry, you may turn your girdle" (or "you may turn the buckle of your girdle behind you") is old conventional phrase which seems to mean: "You may remain angry, for aught I care, until you see fit to change your mind." It implies that the speaker feels no concern about the matter. 139. **how:** in whatsoever way. **—with what:** with whatsoever weapons. 139–40. **Do me right:** Accept my challenge. **—protest your cowardice:** proclaim the fact that you are a coward. 142. **so I may have good cheer:** provided I may count on good fare. Claudio speaks as if he had been invited to a feast. He can hardly take Benedick's challenge seriously. 144. **bid me:** invited me. **—to a calve's head:** to a duel with a foolish fellow. 145. **curiously:** elaborately, skillfully. **—naught:** good for nothing. 146. **find:** i.e., as part of the bill of fare. **—a woodcock.** Claudio is at a loss to understand Benedick's anger. The woodcock (though in fact an intelligent bird) was regarded as particularly stupid; it was even thought to have no brains. They are still at cross purposes. Claudio cannot understand why he has been challenged; Don Pedro, who cannot imagine that Benedick is serious, continues in a jesting vein, with intent to further the projected match between Beatrice and Benedick, and Claudio goes on in the same tenor.

---

†   Benedick's challenge marks his public break with his comrades. How seriously they take him varies from production to production. In Burge's film, Claudio senses Benedick's earnestness before Don Pedro, and Don Pedro's continued jesting strikes a discordant note.

BENEDICK   Sir, your wit ambles well; it goes easily.

DON PEDRO   I'll tell thee how Beatrice prais'd thy wit the other day. I said thou
hadst a fine wit: "True," said she, "a fine little one." "No," said I, "a
great wit." "Right," says she, "a great gross one." "Nay," said   150
I, "a good wit." "Just," said she, "it hurts nobody." "Nay," said I,
"the gentleman is wise." "Certain," said she, "a wise gentleman."
"Nay," said I, "he hath the tongues." "That I believe," said she, "for
he swore a thing to me on Monday night which he forswore on
Tuesday morning. There's a double tongue; there's two tongues."
Thus did she an hour together transshape thy particular virtues.
Yet at last she concluded with a sigh, thou wast the proper'st man
in Italy.

CLAUDIO   For the which she wept heartily and said she cared not.   159

DON PEDRO   Yea, that she did; but yet, for all that, an if she did not hate him
deadly, she would love him dearly. The old man's daughter told us
all.

CLAUDIO   All, all! and moreover, God saw him when he was hid in the
garden.

DON PEDRO   But when shall we set the savage bull's horns on the sensible   165
Benedick's head?

CLAUDIO   Yea, and text underneath, "Here dwells Benedick, the married
man"?

BENEDICK   Fare you well, boy; you know my mind. I will leave you now to
your gossiplike humor. You break jests as braggards do their   170
blades, which God be thanked hurt not. My lord, for your many
courtesies I thank you. I must discontinue your company. Your
brother the bastard is fled from Messina. You have among you

---

150. **a great gross one:** a great one, if by "great" you mean "coarse," "stupid." 151. **Just:** just so; quite
right. 152. **a wise gentleman:** wise enough for a *gentleman*. Spoken with ironical emphasis: "No doubt
he has all the wisdom we can expect of a *gentleman*!" 153. **he hath the tongues:** he is well versed in
foreign languages. 154. **forswore:** denied with an oath. 155. **double:** deceitful. 156. **thy particular:**
thy own personal. 157. **proper'st:** handsomest. 163–64. **God saw him...garden.** See *Genesis*, iii, 8.
Benedick is too angry to see the point. 165–66. **When...head?** When shall we see Benedick married?
Once more the everlasting jest about the cuckold's horns. 167. **Yea, and text underneath:** Yes, and
when shall we write, "in great letters" under his picture,...Claudio is echoing Benedick's defiant words
in 1.1 "Let me be vilely painted, and in such great letters as they write 'Here is good horse to hire,' let
them signify under my sign 'Here you may see Benedick the married man.'" 169. **you know my mind:**
You know what I think of you, and what I am ready to do in order to prove that I am right in my
opinion. 169–70. **I will leave you...humor:** I'll leave you to the enjoyment of your whimsical frame of
mind, which is about as sensible as that of a chattering old woman. —**break jests:** make jokes at other
persons' expense. 170–71. **as braggarts do their blades:** i.e., in sham fights, undertaken merely to show
off and involving no danger.

kill'd a sweet and innocent lady. For my Lord Lackbeard there, he
and I shall meet; and till then peace be with him.   [*Exit.*] 175

DON PEDRO   He is in earnest.

CLAUDIO   In most profound earnest; and, I'll warrant you, for the love of
Beatrice.

DON PEDRO   And hath challeng'd thee.

CLAUDIO   Most sincerely.   180

DON PEDRO   What a pretty thing man is when he goes in his doublet and hose
and leaves off his wit!

Enter Constables [Dogberry and Verges, with the Watch, leading]
Conrade and Borachio.

CLAUDIO   He is then a giant to an ape; but then is an ape a doctor to such a
man.

DON PEDRO   But, soft you, let me be! Pluck up, my heart, and be sad! Did he
not say my brother was fled?   186

DOGBERRY   Come you, sir. If justice cannot tame you, she shall ne'er weigh
more reasons in her balance. Nay, an you be a cursing hypocrite
once, you must be look'd to.

DON PEDRO   How now? two of my brother's men bound? Borachio one.   190

CLAUDIO   Hearken after their offence, my lord.

DON PEDRO   Officers, what offence have these men done?

DOGBERRY   Marry, sir, they have committed false report; moreover, they have
spoken untruths; secondarily, they are slanders; sixth and lastly,
they have belied a lady; thirdly, they have verified unjust things;
and to conclude, they are lying knaves.   196

DON PEDRO   First, I ask thee what they have done; thirdly, I ask thee what's
their offence; sixth and lastly, why they are committed; and to
conclude, what you lay to their charge.

---

174. **For:** as for. —**my Lord Lackbeard.** Cf. Antonio's "sir boy." 175. **meet:** in a duel (for I have
challenged him). 179. **hath challeng'd thee.** Don Pedro did not hear what Benedick said to Claudio
earlier. 181–82. **What...wit!** What a figure a man makes when he walks about in his ordinary attire
but has neglected to put on his common sense along with his clothes! 183. **He is then a giant to an
ape:** Then (when he has forgotten to put on his wits along with his clothes) he is, no doubt, a giant in
stature in comparison with an ape; but, to tell the truth, an ape—silly creature as he is—is a wise man in
comparison with such a fellow. —**a doctor:** a learned scholar. 185. **soft you:** literally, "go slow," "don't
be in a hurry." —**Pluck up, my heart, and be sad!** Pull up, my dear fellow, and be serious. 187–88.
she shall ne'er weigh more reasons in her balance: she will nevermore be able to weigh law cases in
her scales. Dogberry misuses *reasons* (which often means "causes") in the sense of "cases at law." —**a
cursing hypocrite.** Dogberry seems to mean "a lying impostor." 195. **verified:** asserted as true. 198.
committed: arrested and held for trial.

CLAUDIO	Rightly reasoned, and in his own division; and by my troth there's one meaning well suited. 201
DON PEDRO	Who have you offended, masters, that you are thus bound to your answer? This learned constable is too cunning to be understood. What's your offence? 204
BORACHIO	Sweet Prince, let me go no farther to mine answer. Do you hear me, and let this Count kill me. I have deceived even your very eyes. What your wisdoms could not discover, these shallow fools have brought to light, who in the night overheard me confessing to this man, how Don John your brother incensed me to slander the Lady Hero; how you were brought into the orchard and saw me court Margaret in Hero's garments; how you disgrac'd her when you should marry her. My villainy they have upon record, which I had rather seal with my death than repeat over to my shame. The lady is dead upon mine and my master's false accusation; and briefly, I desire nothing but the reward of a villain. 215
DON PEDRO	Runs not this speech like iron through your blood?
CLAUDIO	I have drunk poison whiles he utter'd it.
DON PEDRO	But did my brother set thee on to this?
BORACHIO	Yea, and paid me richly for the practice of it.
DON PEDRO	He is compos'd and fram'd of treachery, 220 And fled he is upon this villainy.
CLAUDIO	Sweet Hero, now thy image doth appear In the rare semblance that I lov'd it first.
DOGBERRY	Come, bring away the plaintiffs. By this time our sexton hath reformed Signior Leonato of the matter. And, masters, do not 225 forget to specify, when time and place shall serve, that I am an ass.
VERGES	Here, here comes Master Signior Leonato, and the sexton too.

Enter Leonato, his brother [Antonio], and the Sexton.

LEONATO	Which is the villain? Let me see his eyes, That, when I note another man like him, I may avoid him. Which of these is he? 230

---

200. **division:** method of dividing up and arranging the subject matter. 201. **one meaning well suited:** one single idea dressed up in becoming terms. 203. **too cunning:** too subtle in his language. 205. **let me go no farther to mine answer:** Let me confess and be punished here and now. *Answer* is used in two senses: (1) answer to your question and (2) answering for my crime (paying the penalty). 209. **incensed:** incited, instigated. 210. **orchard:** garden. 211–12. **when you should marry her:** when you were to marry her. —**upon:** as the result of. 219. **for the practice of it:** for forming and carrying out the plot. 224. **plaintiffs:** for "defendants." 225. **reformed:** for "informed."

BORACHIO	If you would know your wronger, look on me.
LEONATO	Art thou the slave that with thy breath hast kill'd Mine innocent child?
BORACHIO	Yea, even I alone.
LEONATO	No, not so, villain! thou beliest thyself. Here stand a pair of honorable men— 235 A third is fled—that had a hand in it. I thank you princes for my daughter's death. Record it with your high and worthy deeds. 'Twas bravely done, if you bethink you of it.
CLAUDIO	I know not how to pray your patience; 240 Yet I must speak. Choose your revenge yourself; Impose me to what penance your invention Can lay upon my sin. Yet sinn'd I not But in mistaking.
DON PEDRO	By my soul, nor I! And yet, to satisfy this good old man, 245 I would bend under any heavy weight That he'll enjoin me to.
LEONATO	I cannot bid you bid my daughter live— That were impossible; but I pray you both, Possess the people in Messina here 250 How innocent she died; and if your love Can labor aught in sad invention, Hang her an epitaph upon her tomb, And sing it to her bones—sing it tonight. Tomorrow morning come you to my house, 255 And since you could not be my son-in-law, Be yet my nephew. My brother hath a daughter, Almost the copy of my child that's dead, And she alone is heir to both of us. Give her the right you should have giv'n her cousin, 260 And so dies my revenge.
CLAUDIO	O noble sir! Your over-kindness doth wring tears from me.

---

239. **'Twas bravely done:** It was a magnificent act. 240. **to pray your patience:** to beg you to hear me calmly. 242. **Impose me to:** appoint me to; sentence me to. 250. **Possess:** inform. 259. **she alone is heir to both of us.** But, as a matter of fact, Antonio has a son (see 1.2). The inconsistency is not explained by supposing that Leonato's statement is "part of his fiction"; for that son is not away from home, and Leonato's guests must have made his acquaintance already. 260. **should have giv'n:** were to give.

I do embrace your offer; and dispose
For henceforth of poor Claudio.

LEONATO   Tomorrow then I will expect your coming;   265
Tonight I take my leave. This naughty man
Shall face to face be brought to Margaret,
Who I believe was pack'd in all this wrong,
Hir'd to it by your brother.

BORACHIO   No, by my soul, she was not;
Nor knew not what she did when she spoke to me;   270
But always hath been just and virtuous
In anything that I do know by her.

DOGBERRY   Moreover, sir, which indeed is not under white and black, this
plaintiff here, the offender, did call me ass. I beseech you let it be
rememb'red in his punishment. And also the watch heard them
talk of one Deformed. They say he wears a key in his ear, and a
lock hanging by it, and borrows money in God's name, the which
he hath us'd so long and never paid that now men grow hard-
hearted and will lend nothing for God's sake. Pray you examine
him upon that point.   280

LEONATO   I thank thee for thy care and honest pains.

DOGBERRY   Your worship speaks like a most thankful and reverent youth, and
I praise God for you.

LEONATO   There's for thy pains. [*Gives money.*]

DOGBERRY   God save the foundation!   285

LEONATO   Go, I discharge thee of thy prisoner, and I thank thee.

DOGBERRY   I leave an arrant knave with your worship, which I beseech your
worship to correct yourself, for the example of others. God keep
your worship! I wish your worship well. God restore you to health!
I humbly give you leave to depart; and if a merry meeting may be
wish'd, God prohibit it! Come, neighbor.   291

---

263. **dispose.** Not "I dispose" but "dispose you" (imperative). "I am your humble servant to dispose
of as you will." 267. **pack'd in all this wrong:** an accomplice in this whole conspiracy. *Packing* is a
synonym for "plotting." 271. **just:** good, righteous. 272. **by her:** about her. 273. **not under white and
black:** not "written down" in black and white. 276. **a key.** Doubtless the "lock" (see note 3.3.131)
suggested the key to Dogberry's logical mind. 277. **borrows money in God's name:** like a beggar, who
asks alms "for God's sake." —**the which...so long:** which habit he has so long practiced. 279. **nothing:**
i.e., either to him or to anybody. 282. **reverent.** Probably Dogberry actually means "reverent," though
the word is very common in the sense of "reverend." 285. **God save the foundation!** Such was the
customary phrase employed by those who received alms at the gates of religious houses. It was really
a prayer for the soul of the founder of the house and for God's blessing on the establishment. 286.
I discharge thee of thy prisoner: I free thee from further responsibility for him. Leonato, being a
magistrate, takes charge of the prisoner. 290–91. **if...prohibit it!** Doubtless he means, "God grant we
may meet again on a more cheerful occasion!"

Exeunt [Dogberry and Verges].

LEONATO   Until tomorrow morning, lords, farewell.

ANTONIO   Farewell, my lords. We look for you tomorrow.

DON PEDRO   We will not fail.

CLAUDIO   Tonight I'll mourn with Hero.

[Exeunt Don Pedro and Claudio.]

LEONATO   *[to the Watch]* Bring you these fellows on.—We'll talk with Margaret,
            How her acquaintance grew with this lewd fellow.   *Exeunt.* 296

SCENE II. [Leonato's *orchard.*]

Enter Benedick and Margaret [meeting].

BENEDICK   Pray thee, sweet Mistress Margaret, deserve well at my hands by
            helping me to the speech of Beatrice.

MARGARET   Will you then write me a sonnet in praise of my beauty?

BENEDICK   In so high a style, Margaret, that no man living shall come over it;
            for in most comely truth thou deservest it.   5

MARGARET   To have no man come over me? Why, shall I always keep below
            stairs?

BENEDICK   Thy wit is as quick as the greyhound's mouth—it catches.

MARGARET   And yours as blunt as the fencer's foils, which hit but hurt not.

BENEDICK   A most manly wit, Margaret: it will not hurt a woman. And so I
            pray thee call Beatrice. I give thee the bucklers.   11

MARGARET   Give us the swords; we have bucklers of our own.

BENEDICK   If you use them, Margaret, you must put in the pikes with a vice,
            and they are dangerous weapons for maids.

MARGARET   Well, I will call Beatrice to you, who I think hath legs.   15

BENEDICK   And therefore will come.   *Exit Margaret.*

---

296. **lewd.** In the old general sense: "low," "disreputable."
SCENE II.
5. **for...deservest it:** for only the most exalted style can do justice to thy beauty—can describe it as
it actually is. 6–7. **keep below stairs:** remain down stairs—in the servants' quarters. 9. **blunt...foils.**
Fencing foils were blunted but had no button on the point. 11. **I give thee the bucklers:** I yield; I lay
aside all thoughts of defense. The *buckler* was a kind of shield. 13. **the pikes.** A buckler had a pointed
spike in the centre. **—a vice:** a screw.

[*Sings.*] The god of love,
    That sits above
And knows me, and knows me,
    How pitiful I deserve—   20

I mean in singing; but in loving Leander the good swimmer,
Troilus the first employer of panders, and a whole book full of
these quondam carpet-mongers, whose names yet run smoothly
in the even road of a blank verse—why, they were never so truly
turn'd over and over as my poor self in love. Marry, I cannot   25
show it in rhyme. I have tried. I can find out no rhyme to "lady"
but "baby"—an innocent rhyme; for "scorn," "horn"—a hard
rhyme; for "school," "fool"—a babbling rhyme: very ominous
endings! No, I was not born under a rhyming planet, nor I cannot
woo in festival terms.   30

Enter Beatrice.

Sweet Beatrice, wouldst thou come when I call'd thee?

BEATRICE   Yea, signior, and depart when you bid me.

BENEDICK   O, stay but till then!

BEATRICE   'Then' is spoken. Fare you well now. And yet, ere I go, let me go
with that I came for, which is, with knowing what hath pass'd   35
between you and Claudio.

BENEDICK   Only foul words; and thereupon I will kiss thee.

BEATRICE   Foul words is but foul wind, and foul wind is but foul breath, and
foul breath is noisome. Therefore I will depart unkiss'd.   39

BENEDICK   Thou hast frighted the word out of his right sense, so forcible is thy
wit. But I must tell thee plainly, Claudio undergoes my challenge;

17–20. **The God of love, etc.:** The beginning of a song by William Elderton, a popular ballad-writer of
Shakespeare's time. —**How pitiful I deserve:** This means "How much I deserve pity (for my unrequited
affection)"; but Benedick interprets it in the sense of "How slight my deserts are" and protests that,
though he may be without merit as a singer, he is the greatest lover on record. 21. **Leander.** According
to legend, Leander was the beloved of Hero; he died swimming across the Hellespont to be with her, and
has thus been held as an example of dedication and fidelity. As discussed in the Introduction, (p.xiv),
Shakespeare pointedly does not name the beloved of Hero in *Much Ado* Leander, but rather something
less distinguished, Claudio. [P.K.] 22. **panders.** The word is derived from the name of Pandarus.
Compare his speech in *Troilus and Cressida,* 3.2.: "If ever you prove false one to another, since I have
taken such pain to bring you together, let all pitiful goers-between be call'd to the world's end after
my name; call them all Pandars. Let all constant men be Troiluses, all false women Cressids, and all
brokers-between Pandars!" 23. **quondam:** ancient. —**carpet-mongers.** *Carpet knight* is an old satirical
term for one who has been dubbed knight without having done military service. Benedick applies a
similar term to all the famous lovers of antiquity, for, he asserts, they were only triflers in comparison
with himself. 25. **Marry:** to be sure; true enough. 27. **innocent:** childish. 37. **thereupon:** on account of
that—i.e., I claim a kiss as my reward for challenging him. 40. **his right sense:** its proper meaning. The
pun on *sense* is obvious. 41. **undergoes:** has been subjected to.

and either I must shortly hear from him or I will subscribe him a coward. And I pray thee now tell me, for which of my bad parts didst thou first fall in love with me?   44

BEATRICE   For them all together, which maintain'd so politic a state of evil that they will not admit any good part to intermingle with them. But for which of my good parts did you first suffer love for me?

BENEDICK   Suffer love!—a good epithet. I do suffer love indeed, for I love thee against my will.   49

BEATRICE   In spite of your heart, I think. Alas, poor heart! If you spite it for my sake, I will spite it for yours, for I will never love that which my friend hates.

BENEDICK   Thou and I are too wise to woo peaceably.

BEATRICE   It appears not in this confession. There's not one wise man among twenty that will praise himself.   55

BENEDICK   An old, an old instance, Beatrice, that liv'd in the time of good neighbors. If a man do not erect in this age his own tomb ere he dies, he shall live no longer in monument than the bell rings and the widow weeps.

BEATRICE   And how long is that, think you?   60

BENEDICK   Question: why, an hour in clamor and a quarter in rheum. Therefore is it most expedient for the wise, if Don Worm (his conscience) find no impediment to the contrary, to be the trumpet of his own virtues, as I am to myself. So much for praising myself, who, I myself will bear witness, is praiseworthy. And now tell me, how doth your cousin?   66

BEATRICE   Very ill.

BENEDICK   And how do you?

BEATRICE   Very ill too.   69

42–43. **subscribe him a coward:** "post" him in some public place as a coward (with my signature attached to the notice). —**parts:** qualities. 45. **maintain'd...evil:** maintain'd so well organized a condition of badness. The use of *politic* shows that there is a shadowy pun on *state* in the sense of "a political organization." 48. **epithet:** phrase. 54. **It appears not in this confession:** This declaration— that you are wise—does not show wisdom, for self-praise is not a wise man's habit. —**confession.** Used as in the phrase "confession of faith." 56–57. **old instance...neighbors:** That maxim about self-praise that you quote is an obsolete doctrine. It was current—and had some truth in it—in the good old times, when a man's neighbors were ready to commend his good qualities. 58. **live no longer in monument:** have no monument that shall keep his memory alive. 61. **Question:** "A problem," says Benedick, "but an easy one to solve." —**clamour:** the mournful sound of the bell. —**rheum:** tears. 62–63. **Don Worm (his conscience).** conscience was desribed as a worm that gnawed away at the soul.

BENEDICK	Serve God, love me, and mend. There will I leave you too, for here comes one in haste.

Enter Ursula.

URSULA	Madam, you must come to your uncle. Yonder's old coil at home. It is proved my Lady Hero hath been falsely accus'd, the Prince and Claudio mightily abus'd, and Don John is the author of all, who is fled and gone. Will you come presently? 75
BEATRICE	Will you go hear this news, signior?
BENEDICK	I will live in thy heart, die in thy lap, and be buried in thy eyes; and moreover, I will go with thee to thy uncle's. *Exeunt.*

SCENE III. [*A churchyard.*]

Enter Claudio, Don Pedro, and three or four with tapers, [followed by Musicians].†

CLAUDIO	Is this the monument of Leonato?
LORD	It is, my lord.
CLAUDIO	[*reads from a scroll*]

    Epitaph.

        Done to death by slanderous tongues
           Was the Hero that here lies.
        Death, in guerdon of her wrongs,   5
           Gives her fame which never dies.
        So the life that died with shame
        Lives in death with glorious fame.

    Hang thou there upon the tomb,   [*Hangs up the scroll.*]
    Praising her when I am dumb.   10
    Now, music, sound, and sing your solemn hymn.

---

70. **mend:** recover from your illness. Benedick implies that his prescription ("Serve God, love me") will effect a rapid recovery. —**There will I leave you too:** With that advice I'll say good-bye. 72. **old coil:** a great hubbub. 74. **abus'd:** deceived.
SCENE III.
5. **guerdon:** reward or recompense. 7. **with:** because of. 10. **when I am dumb:** when I am dead and can praise her no longer.

---

†   In the BBC film, Claudio, Don Pedro and the other mourners enter a tiled chamber wearing dark robes and carrying torches; they come and go rather formally and quickly, allowing themselves only the time it takes to speak and sing the text. In Antoon's version, a much larger crowd gathers at a graveside in a churchyard, under umbrellas in the rain; they remain through the night until dawn, then disperse. Branagh's is the most elaborate: a torch-lit procession winds along a road at night, until it reaches the gated entrance to Hero's tomb; Claudio reads the epitaph with deep emotion, breaking into tears as Balthasar sings, "Pardon, goddess of the night." [P.K.]

Song.

Pardon, goddess of the night,
Those that slew thy virgin knight;
For the which, with songs of woe,
Round about her tomb they go.   15
  Midnight, assist our moan,
  Help us to sigh and groan
    Heavily, heavily.
Graves, yawn and yield your dead,
Till death be uttered   20
    Heavily, heavily.

CLAUDIO   Now unto thy bones good night!
Yearly will I do this rite.

DON PEDRO   Good morrow, masters. Put your torches out.
The wolves have prey'd, and look, the gentle day,   25
Before the wheels of Phœbus, round about
Dapples the drowsy east with spots of grey.
Thanks to you all, and leave us. Fare you well.

CLAUDIO   Good morrow, masters. Each his several way.

DON PEDRO   Come, let us hence and put on other weeds,   30
And then to Leonato's we will go.

CLAUDIO   And Hymen now with luckier issue speeds
Than this for whom we rend'red up this woe.   *Exeunt.*

SCENE IV. [*The hall in Leonato's house.*]

---

*Enter Leonato, Benedick, [Beatrice,] Margaret,
Ursula, Antonio, Friar [Francis], Hero.*

FRIAR   Did I not tell you she was innocent?

LEONATO   So are the Prince and Claudio, who accus'd her
Upon the error that you heard debated.
But Margaret was in some fault for this,
Although against her will, as it appears   5

---

12. **goddess of the night:** Diana, the moon goddess and the patron deity of maidens. 13. **thy virgin knight.** As a maiden, Hero died a devotee of Diana. [P.K.] 18. **heavily:** mournfully. 19–20. **yield your dead...uttered:** release your dead that they may join with us in our mourning until her death has been lamented to the full. 25. **The wolves have prey'd:** have finished their prowling, since dawn is at hand. 26. **Phœbus:** In mythology, Phœbus (Apollo) drove the chariot of the sun. 30. **weeds:** garments. 32–33. **Hymen...woe:** A marriage is now at hand which is to have a more fortunate outcome than hers for whom we are here mourning. (Hymen was the Greek god of marriage.)
SCENE IV.

Claudio and Don Pedro watch the break of day at Hero's tomb in Antoon's *Much Ado*. (1973)

	In the true course of all the question.	
ANTONIO	Well, I am glad that all things sort so well.	
BENEDICK	And so am I, being else by faith enforc'd To call young Claudio to a reckoning for it.	
LEONATO	Well, daughter, and you gentlewomen all, Withdraw into a chamber by yourselves, And when I send for you, come hither mask'd. *Exeunt Ladies.* The Prince and Claudio promis'd by this hour To visit me. You know your office, brother: You must be father to your brother's daughter, And give her to young Claudio.	10 15
ANTONIO	Which I will do with confirm'd countenance.	
BENEDICK	Friar, I must entreat your pains, I think.	
FRIAR	To do what, signior?	
BENEDICK	To bind me, or undo me—one of them. Signior Leonato, truth it is, good signior, Your niece regards me with an eye of favor.	20
LEONATO	That eye my daughter lent her. 'Tis most true.	

3. **Upon:** because of. **in some fault:** somewhat to blame. 5. **against her will:** unintentionally 6. **question:** investigation. 7. **sort:** come out, result. 8. **faith:** fidelity to my promise. 14. **your office:** your duty; the part you have to act. 17. **with cónfirm'd countenance:** with steadfast looks and demeanor. *Countenance* often means "bearing," "behavior." It is not confined to "expression of the face." 20. **undo:** ruin—with an obvious pun.

BENEDICK	And I do with an eye of love requite her.
LEONATO	The sight whereof I think you had from me, 25 From Claudio, and the Prince; but what's your will?
BENEDICK	Your answer, sir, is enigmatical; But, for my will, my will is, your good will May stand with ours, this day to be conjoin'd In the state of honorable marriage; 30 In which, good friar, I shall desire your help.
LEONATO	My heart is with your liking.
FRIAR	And my help.

Enter Don Pedro and Claudio and two or three other.

Here comes the Prince and Claudio.

DON PEDRO	Good morrow to this fair assembly.
LEONATO	Good morrow, Prince; good morrow, Claudio. 35 We here attend you. Are you yet determin'd Today to marry with my brother's daughter?
CLAUDIO	I'll hold my mind, were she an Ethiope.
LEONATO	Call her forth, brother. Here's the friar ready. [*Exit Antonio.*]
DON PEDRO	Good morrow, Benedick. Why, what's the matter 40 That you have such a February face, So full of frost, of storm, and cloudiness?
CLAUDIO	I think he thinks upon the savage bull. Tush, fear not, man! We'll tip thy horns with gold, And all Europa shall rejoice at thee, 45 As once Europa did at lusty Jove When he would play the noble beast in love.
BENEDICK	Bull Jove, sir, had an amiable low, And some such strange bull leap'd your father's cow And got a calf in that same noble feat 50 Much like to you, for you have just his bleat.

Enter [Leonato's] brother [Antonio], Hero, Beatrice, Margaret,
Ursula, [the ladies wearing masks].†

25–26. **The sight…Prince.** Since his love, Leonato thinks, was the result of his overhearing the conversation in 2.3. 29. **stand with:** agree with. 38. **Ethiope:** of dark complexion, considered unattractive in Shakespeare's time. (see note 2.1.248) 41. **a February face.** coldness and reserve. 45. **Europa:** Europe. The tale of Jupiter and Europa, in which Jupiter seduced the maiden in the form of a bull, was one of the most popular of all mythological love-stories.

---

†   A carousel is the centerpiece of Antoon's staging of this scene, the masked ladies riding on ponies, adding to the festive nature of the dénouement.[P.K.]

CLAUDIO	For this I owe you. Here comes other reck'nings.
	Which is the lady I must seize upon?
ANTONIO	This same is she, and I do give you her.
CLAUDIO	Why then, she's mine. Sweet, let me see your face. 55
LEONATO	No, that you shall not till you take her hand
	Before this friar and swear to marry her.
CLAUDIO	Give me your hand before this holy friar.
	I am your husband if you like of me.
HERO	And when I liv'd I was your other wife; [*Unmasks.*] 60
	And when you lov'd you were my other husband.
CLAUDIO	Another Hero!
HERO	Nothing certainer.
	One Hero died defil'd; but I do live,
	And surely as I live, I am a maid.
DON PEDRO	The former Hero! Hero that is dead! 65
LEONATO	She died, my lord, but whiles her slander liv'd.
FRIAR	All this amazement can I qualify,
	When, after that the holy rites are ended,
	I'll tell you largely of fair Hero's death.
	Meantime let wonder seem familiar, 70
	And to the chapel let us presently.
BENEDICK	Soft and fair, friar. Which is Beatrice?
BEATRICE	[*unmasks*] I answer to that name.
	What is your will?
BENEDICK	Do not you love me?
BEATRICE	Why, no; no more than reason. 75
BENEDICK	Why, then your uncle, and the Prince, and Claudio
	Have been deceived; for they swore you did.
BEATRICE	Do not you love me?
BENEDICK	Troth, no; no more than reason.
BEATRICE	Why, then my cousin, Margaret, and Ursula
	Are much deceiv'd; for they did swear you did. 80

52. **For this I owe you. Here comes other reck'nings:** I must postpone the payment of that gibe of yours. Here come other accounts that I must settle first. 63. **defil'd** disgraced. 67. **qualify:** modify, lessen, relieve. 69. **largely:** in full. 70. **let wonder seem familiar:** treat all these marvels as if they were ordinary matters; do not let them disturb you. 72. **Soft and fair:** Wait a moment—literally, Go slowly and easily. 78. **Troth:** by my faith.

BENEDICK	They swore that you were almost sick for me.
BEATRICE	They swore that you were well-nigh dead for me.
BENEDICK	'Tis no such matter. Then you do not love me?
BEATRICE	No, truly, but in friendly recompense.
LEONATO	Come, cousin, I am sure you love the gentleman. 85
CLAUDIO	And I'll be sworn upon't that he loves her;
	For here's a paper written in his hand,
	A halting sonnet of his own pure brain,
	Fashion'd to Beatrice.
HERO	And here's another,
	Writ in my cousin's hand, stol'n from her pocket, 90
	Containing her affection unto Benedick.
BENEDICK	A miracle! Here's our own hands against our hearts. Come, I will have thee; but, by this light, I take thee for pity.
BEATRICE	I would not deny you; but, by this good day, I yield upon great persuasion, and partly to save your life, for I was told you were in a consumption. 96
BENEDICK	Peace! I will stop your mouth. [*Kisses her.*]
DON PEDRO	How dost thou, Benedick, the married man?
BENEDICK	I'll tell thee what, Prince: a college of wit-crackers cannot flout me out of my humor. Dost thou think I care for a satire or an 100 epigram? No. If a man will be beaten with brains, 'a shall wear nothing handsome about him. In brief, since I do purpose to marry, I will think nothing to any purpose that the world can say against it; and therefore never flout at me for what I have said against it; for man is a giddy thing, and this is my conclusion. For thy part, Claudio, I did think to have beaten thee; but in that thou art like to be my kinsman, live unbruis'd, and love my cousin.

---

83. **no such matter:** nothing of the kind. 84. **but...recompense:** only as a friend loves a friend. 85. **cousin:** niece. 88. **halting:** limping. Despite his confessed lack of skill in rhyming (5.2) Benedick has so far yielded to custom as to compose a love sonnet, but he has not ventured to show it to Beatrice. —**of his own pure brain:** purely of his own invention. 92. **Here's...hearts:** Here is our own handwriting to give evidence to prove our hearts guilty of love. 95–96. **in a consumption:** in a decline—wasting away with lovesickness. 99. **wit-crackers:** fellows who crack jokes. —**flout:** jeer. 100. **my humor:** my fancy. 101–02. **If a man...him:** No man who is so weak as to allow mere witticisms to give him a thrashing will ever be able to wear good clothes without having them spoiled by beating. 103. **I will think nothing to any purpose:** I will regard nothing as of any consequence. 105. **this is my conclusion:** this is my final purpose.

Beatrice and Benedick discover what each has written in secret. (Branagh, 1993)

CLAUDIO   I had well hop'd thou wouldst have denied Beatrice, that I might
have cudgell'd thee out of thy single life, to make thee a double-
dealer, which out of question thou wilt be if my cousin do not look
exceeding narrowly to thee.   111

BENEDICK   Come, come, we are friends. Let's have a dance ere we are married,
that we may lighten our own hearts and our wives' heels.

LEONATO   We'll have dancing afterward.   114

BENEDICK   First, of my word! Therefore play, music. Prince, thou art sad. Get
thee a wife, get thee a wife! There is no staff more reverent than
one tipp'd with horn.

Enter Messenger.

MESSENGER My lord, your brother John is ta'en in flight,
And brought with armed men back to Messina.

BENEDICK   Think not on him till tomorrow. I'll devise thee brave   120
punishments for him. Strike up, pipers!   *Dance. [Exeunt.]*‡

109–10. **a double-dealer.** The pun is complicated, but obvious enough: "To make thee cease to be a
'single man' by forcing thee to marry—and that would make thee a double-dealer, since I am sure thou
wilt be an unfaithful husband unless," etc. 115. **of my word!** on my word! 116. **staff:** walking stick.
—**reverent:** reverend, worthy of honor. A final joke about the cuckold's horns. 118. **ta'en in flight.** has
been apprehended while fleeing. [P.K.]. 120. **brave:** fine, splendid.

---

‡   Branagh's film ends with a reprise of "Hey, nonny, nonny," as the cast joyfully dances through the
gardens of the estate; the full scope of film production over stage is evident, as an orchestra plays,
a chorus sings, and the camera slowly rises higher and higher, panning over the strands of dancers
and finally looking out over the surrounding Tuscan hills. [P.K.]

How to Read *Much Ado About Nothing* as Performance

Suit the word to the action

Although we often think of Shakespeare's plays as falling under the category of "literature," Shakespeare did not see his work this way. As far as we know, he never sought to publish his dramatic works in the same way that he did his narrative poems. Like other dramatists of his period, Shakespeare assumed that his plays would be encountered on the stage, not on the page. It enriches our experience of reading Shakespeare, therefore, to bear in mind that they are blueprints for performance. Shakespeare's characters, after all, are simply lines on a page. They may have come to life in thousands of different incarnations, on stage and on film, but insofar as they persist, they do so through the words that Shakespeare has written for actors to speak. Whether played by Richard Burbage in Shakespeare's day, David Garrick in the eighteenth century, or Kenneth Branagh in a twentieth-century film, Benedick *is* what Benedick *says*. Of course, *how* Benedick says what he says is a matter of interpretation, and this is the actor's art. The process of performance thus begins, in the most literal sense, with reading. The following are a few strategies, grounded in a character-based approach to performance that melds what John Barton (co-founder of the Royal Shakespeare Company) calls the "two traditions" of Shakespearean acting—the Renaissance and modern approaches to the text—intended to help you read Shakespeare as one might when preparing to stage his plays.

Everyone according to his cue

In the Elizabethan playhouse, players (what actors were more commonly called) were never presented with an entire play script. Because it was expensive to produce full copies, and because acting companies wanted to keep their own plays out of the hands of other companies and unscrupulous publishers, players would be given only their own parts. These "roles" (so named because they were rolled up into a scroll) contained only a character's own lines, preceded by a short "cue", usually three or so words, that would tell them when they were meant to speak. They were compelled, therefore, to learn their lines without knowing what the other characters were saying, or even how much time would elapse between one of their speeches and the next. Moreover, there was little time for rehearsal, so players would memorize their separate parts, come together for some basic blocking, and then put the play on as quickly as possible. Thus Shakespeare had to build into a character's lines all the information a player would need to undertake their part. Reading those lines as closely as possible will provide the clues necessary to construct an idea of each individual character.

What? Why? How?

There are really just three steps we take when interpreting Shakespeare's characters: *What* exactly does a character say? *Why* are they saying what they're saying? And—and this is where we cross into performance—*how* does he or she speak those lines? To be more explicit, we move from 1) understanding the literal meaning of Shakespeare's words to 2) interpreting those words in the context in which they are found to 3) making choices as to how to convey the truth of those words through speech and action. When Beatrice asks in her first line, "Tell me, has Signor Mountanto returned from these wars or no?"(1.1.23) it is not difficult to understand her; although she expresses herself differently than we might, *what* she says is clear. When the other characters indicate that "Signor Mountanto" is a reference to Benedick, we ask *why* Beatrice would call him by such a name. With the help of the footnotes, which indicate that "Mountanto" is a thinly-veiled insult, indicating, a social climber and, perhaps, a sexual opportunist, we understand that her question is a barbed one. An actor would question why someone would tease someone who wasn't present—someone who, paradoxically, she seems quite concerned about. Does she feel compelled to keep up the pretense that she does not care for Benedick? What might this indicate about their relationship? What might it indicate about the way that she presents herself both to Benedick and the rest of the community? Finding answers to these questions will inform how her lines are spoken and how they are heard; in other words, asking *why* a character says *what* she says will suggest *how* those lines may be performed.

Speak the speech

Shakespeare wrote his plays first and foremost to be heard—in fact, the word "audience" comes from the Latin, *audere*, to hear. Rather than reading *Much Ado* silently, as one would a novel or an essay, speaking the lines aloud will allow you to give them the life that the playwright intended them to have. Moreover, each word will be given its proper due. Take Claudio's line, for example, after Leonato has offered him Hero's hand in marriage, Claudio does not answer Leonato immediately; after Beatrice prompts him, he attempts to explain why: "Silence is the perfectest herald of joy" (2.1.238). Our eyes quickly skim across the line when reading, and we get an idea of what he is saying. But speaking the line aloud, we find ourselves emphasizing certain words over others ("silence," perhaps, and/or "joy); and in hearing that emphasis, we have a stronger sense of what Claudio is conveying. We also find that a word like "perfectest" is a bit tongue-tying. Why did Shakespeare not write "most perfect," which would have been a smoother fit? Is Claudio struggling for the right words to express himself? Are we *supposed* to hear "perfectest" as odd-sounding? Is Claudio's claim trickier than it might seem at first? Or has he coined the "perfectest" word to describe what he is thinking and feeling? Just noticing the sorts of questions that arise when we speak the words will help us to focus more intensely on their implications. Speaking the speech will also help us to hear the voices of individual characters. Shakespeare's plays are so vibrant largely because of the vitality of his characters; each is given a distinct voice, which is then woven together with the others by the playwright the way a symphonic composer winds together parts for different instruments. Don John's vicious nature, for example, is evident as he complains that he is muzzled by his brother: "If I had my mouth, I would bite; if I had my liberty, I would do my liking." (1.3.26-27) Dogberry, insulted by Conrade, shows his prickly pride, undercut by his irregular relationship with the English language: "Dost thou not suspect my place? Dost thou not suspect my years? O that [the Sexton] were here to write me down an ass! But, masters, remember that I am an ass. Though it be not written down, yet forget not that I am an ass." (4.2.60-63) Reading the dialogue of Shakespeare's characters only as printed words flattens the characters out; hearing their voices as they were written for the stage brings them to life.

Commit to the language

Perhaps the most intimidating thing about Shakespeare is his language—it seems unnatural to us in so many ways. Shakespeare can come across as unduly poetic, archaic, even esoteric. His language is often thicker, denser, richer than what we are accustomed to hearing. Yet it is this richness that makes Shakespeare so remarkable. If you have ever read a "modernized" version of a Shakespearean play, or seen a film that "updates" his dialogue, you will undoubtedly understand that it's not just *what* is said, but *how* it is said that is important. Imagine if Hamlet, rather than beginning his most famous soliloquy, "To be or not to be, that is the question," asked instead, "Should I kill myself or not, I wonder...?" Such a "translation," intended to bring clarity, actually makes the character of Hamlet *less* accessible to us. There is a radical difference between the prospect of suicide and questioning the value of existence itself. Strip away the opposition of *being* and *not being*, and Hamlet is a much less philosophical character; and if we lose Hamlet's tortured relationship with thought, then we lose the very thing that is driving Hamlet to contemplate death in the first place. We also lose the magnificent resonance of Shakespeare's poetry. Nestled within Hamlet's "question," is the word "quest"—with perfect pitch, mirroring Hamlet's personal predicament, Shakespeare conflates Hamlet's problem with the solution to his problem. Imagine how an actor playing this part would be enlightened by realizing that Hamlet's *quest* is inseparable from asking *questions*... Similarly, in *Much Ado*, when Claudio, throwing Hero back upon her father, exhorts Leonato, "Give not this rotten orange to your friend," (4.1.27) rather than being put off by a metaphor that seems strange to us, let the language lead you to a more profound understanding of Claudio and his situation by questioning what seems odd: How is it that he now sees the woman he had idolized as a rotten piece of fruit? What associations do we have with fruit and "fallen" women? Or with fruit and sensuality? Such lines of thought will take us deeper into the psyche of the characters speaking these words.

Mind your thees and thous

Scanning any page of *Much Ado*, you will likely encounter very few words that are truly unfamiliar to you. Fortunately, editors have already done most of the heavy lifting, appending notes to explain and unpack strange terms and knotty phrases. Even though it may seem tedious to have to turn to the bottom of the page every few lines, once it becomes habit, you will find it less and less intrusive, in the way that reading subtitles in a foreign film is distracting at first, but second nature after awhile. Moreover, you will find yourself over time having to look away from the lines less frequently. From the notes, you will soon assemble a battery of commonly used "uncommon" words and phrases: "wherefore" (why), "in sooth" (in truth), "betimes" (early), "an" (meaning, "if"), and so forth, that will equip you to tackle Shakespeare's work. A few rules of Elizabethan usage will fill out your understanding. Based on pronunciation from the period, "he" is often written as "a." And although it seems counterintuitive to us, "thee" and "thou" are less formal ways of addressing another person than "you." "Thee" and "thou" are used between intimate and familiar characters (friends, lovers, etc.) and from a character of higher social standing towards one of lower (a nobleman to a servant, or a parent to a child). "You" is more formal, used towards one's superiors or in situations demanding decorum. Other rules of usage are made clear in the notes to the play, but you will find that, for the most part, that Elizabethans used English very much as we do.

Prose and Poetry

Shakespeare wrote his plays in both verse and prose, each form serving a different function. Shakespeare's verse, usually ten-syllable lines of poetry, characterized by alternating unstressed and stressed beats ('iambic pentameter' or, when unrhymed, 'blank verse'), was used for speech that was formal, elevated and/or emotionally-charged. Prose was generally used for speech that was more casual, rational, and/or comical. An Elizabethan actor, therefore, would be able to sense from the shape of the language something of the psychological and/or emotional state of his character. Beatrice and Benedick, for example, banter exclusively in prose in the first few scenes, indicating that wit predominates for them over sentiment—or that they are more concerned with being clever than honest. In contrast, the moment that Claudio first expresses to Don Pedro his feelings for Hero, he switches from the prose of their prior conversation to verse, showing quite literally the lyrical nature of love and how it has changed him. Similarly, if Beatrice and Benedick are to become converts to love, we should expect their transformation to be evident in the shape of their language. An actor playing Beatrice will in fact note, looking over her lines, that she switches for the first time from prose to verse at a critical moment—when she overhears her friends talking about Benedick's love for her. Thus Beatrice's transformation is indicated quite literally on the page. Significantly, at the parallel moment in the play, when Benedick overhears his own friends discussing Beatrice's "love," Benedick's response remains in prose, indicating to the actor (and audience) that he has not fully committed to the prospect of loving Beatrice—asking *why* is part of the actor's development towards building a character. Staying attuned to the interplay of poetry and prose will give you a more profound and nuanced sense of character.

Think of language as a spectrum

There are times when Shakespeare's language is rather ordinary, and other times when it becomes more complex, or "heightened." "Heightened" is a useful way to think of language that rises, with purpose, to a particular occasion. Language can be elevated in many ways: conceptually (through devices such as metaphor or antithesis), aurally (through the manipulation of sounds by means of assonance, rhyme, etc.), and/or rhythmically (through the imposition of cadence and meter). We should think of Shakespeare's language as inhabiting a spectrum, from the plainest possible usage to the most ornate. Consider the distance between "Look, here she comes," and "O, she is fall'n / Into a pit of ink, that the wide sea / Hath drops too few to wash her clean again, / And salt too little which may season give / To her foul tainted flesh!" (4.1.134-38) The first line conveys information; the latter is an expression of deep emotional distress at an intense point in the action, marshalling a wide range of linguistic tools to give it its charge. Mirroring life, Shakespeare's language is sometimes casual, sometimes formal—as we read his lines, it is important that we allow the words to communicate to us what is at stake at any given moment. Don't we speak differently amongst our friends than we do when giving a public presentation? Don't we expect a love letter to sound unlike the President's State of the Union address? Doesn't a king address a servant more commandingly than he would his wife (and if not, what is the cause?)? Doesn't an avenger assault his enemy with words even before he draws his sword?

Suit the action to the word

Once you begin to determine how the dialogue between characters is unfolding, your imagination will fill in the world around those characters. *Much Ado* has been set in many times and places, from Renaissance Sicily to the nineteenth-century American frontier (see the "*MA* in Performance" and "*MA* on Screen" sections of the Introduction). As you read the play and become accustomed to envisioning the action in your mind's eye, you will also begin to decide upon appropriate settings for a production. Might you want to capture something of the contemporary feel of the sexual politics of Beatrice and Benedick by locating them in a modern situation, perhaps like the *Shakespeare Retold* version, which casts them as anchors on a television news program? Or do you find Beatrice and Benedick to be outsiders in a world that is old-fashioned and patriarchal – and if so, how might that world be materialized on the stage? Costumes, movement, blocking, music, lighting— all the myriad elements that bring Shakespeare's lines to life—will fall into place, imaginatively or literally, once the language is given its due. Shakespeare suited the words to the action; it is our role to suit the action to the words.

TIMELINE

1554   Matteo Bandello's *Novelle* published, a source for *Much Ado About Nothing*.

1564   William Shakespeare is born in Stratford-upon-Avon to John and Mary Shakespeare, likely on April 23rd, the feast of St. George, the patron saint of England.

1567   The opening of the Red Lion Playhouse, the first public theater in England.

1569   Belleforest's *Histoires Tragiques* published, translating Bandello's *Novelle* into French. This is possibly the edition used by Shakespeare.

1576   The Theater, home to the Lord Chamberlain's Men, is opened in Shoreditch, just outside London.

1582   William Shakespeare marries Anne Hathaway.

1592-94 Plague years. All playhouses are closed for reasons of public health. Shakespeare occupied primarily as a poet during this time.

1594   Shakespeare joins the Lord Chamberlain's Men, a company of actors.

1598-99 Conjectured first performances of *Much Ado About Nothing*.

1599   The Globe Playhouse opened, new home of the Lord Chamberlain's Men.

1600   Publication of *Much Ado About Nothing* in quarto.

1603   Death of Queen Elizabeth. James VI of Scotland is crowned King James I of England. The Lord Chamberlain's Men, patronized by the new monarch, become the King's Men.

1608   The King's Men open a second, indoor playhouse, The Blackfriars.

c.1611   Shakespeare retires to Stratford.

1613   First recorded performance of *Much Ado About Nothing*, staged for the wedding festivities of Princess Elizabeth, daughter to James I.

1616   Death of William Shakespeare (April 23rd).

1623   Publication of the First Folio, the first collection of Shakespeare's dramatic works.

TOPICS FOR DISCUSSION AND FURTHER STUDY

1. *Much Ado About Nothing* is set in Sicily, during a period when the island was occupied by foreign powers (Don Pedro is from Aragon, a region of Spain). Does this situation have any bearing on your reading of the play? Is it something that might be used interestingly in performance?

2. While Hero is living under her father's authority, Beatrice appears to be orphaned, taken in by her uncle. How do these circumstances shape each character?

3. At first glance, the two royal brothers, Don Pedro and Don John, seem to be polar opposites: Don Pedro is gracious and gregarious; Don John is brooding and misanthropic. Yet closer inspection reveals that they are not dissimilar in every way. Both take pleasure in scheming and plotting, manipulating those around them. What is it that motivates each brother to act in such a fashion?

4. The name Benedick comes from the Latin, *benedictus*, meaning "blessed." The name Beatrice translates as "the one who blesses." What might this reveal to us about their relationship?

5. The men in the play share associations that group them together—as soldiers returned from a war, conspirators bent on mischief, or watchmen deputized to keep the city safe. Do the women in the play also share common bonds? If so, what binds them to one another?

6. Why does Shakespeare choose not to stage the scene in which Claudio "witnesses" Hero's betrayal? We hear the details, in fact, chiefly from the report of Borachio as he brags to Conrade. What is lost and/or gained by stage productions and films that elect to enact this scene?

7. During the wedding scene (4.1), Margaret, who clearly knows that Hero is innocent, does not speak up in her defense. Why?

8. Dogberry and the Watch provide comic interludes; yet they also uncover what is truly underway in Messina. Why would Shakespeare make these bunglers the means by which the truth is revealed?

9. In the final scene (5.4), Beatrice and Benedick still pretend in public that they do not love one another, until their friends force them to admit the truth by producing love poems written secretly by each. Why do Beatrice and Benedick continue to keep up this pretense? What roles have poems and songs played in revealing truthful sentiments throughout *Much Ado*?

10. How should Claudio be portrayed when he discovers that Hero is still alive? Is he overjoyed? In shock? Ashamed? Notice that he doesn't say anything directly to her after his line, "Another Hero!" How should Hero be presented in this scene? Has she forgiven him? Do *we* forgive him?

BIBLIOGRAPHY

Berger, Harry, Jr. "Against the Sink-a-Pace: Sexual and Family Politics in *Much Ado About Nothing.*" In *Making Trifles of Terrors: Redistributing Complicities in Shakespeare.* Peter Erickson, ed. Stanford: Stanford University Press, 1997.

Berger scrutinizes the uneasy relationship of the male characters in *Much Ado* to marriage, as well as their preference for masculine privilege and camaraderie. He also illustrates the paradoxical position this puts women in, who are seen as both guaranteeing and threatening male honor.

Berry, Ralph. "Problems of Knowing." In *Shakespeare's Comedies: Explorations in Form.* Princeton: Princeton University Press, 1972.

As *Much Ado* centers on the question of "noting," Berry analyzes in detail the obstacles to knowledge that appear over the course of the action.

Bradbrook, M. C. "Much Ado About Nothing." In *Shakespeare: Modern Essays in Criticism.* Leonard F. Dean, ed. Oxford: Oxford University Press, 1967.

Calling *Much Ado* a "comedy of Masks," Bradbrook contends that in contrast to the garrulous Beatrice and Benedick, Claudio and Hero are "silent lovers," who have no way of knowing one another apart from what "seems" to be, and who are thus vulnerable to plots, real and imagined, based on appearances.

Cook, Carol. "'The Sign and Semblance of Her Honor': Reading Gender Differences in *Much Ado About Nothing.*" *PMLA* 101 (1986): 186-202.

Cook reads the play through a psychoanalytic lens. She analyzes the need of the male characters in *Much Ado* to control meaning and looks at the underlying anxieties that this compulsion reveals.

Davis, Walter R. *Twentieth Century Interpretations of* Much Ado About Nothing. Englewood Cliffs: Prentice, 1969.

This collection gathers together many of the most important critical essays on *Much Ado About Nothing* from the first part of the twentieth century.

Dawson, Anthony B. "Much ado about Signifying." *Studies in English Literature* 22 (1982): 211-221.

Noting that the play both begins and ends with messengers, Dawson finds the central concern of *Much Ado* to be one of interpretation. As messages are delivered, overheard, intercepted and so forth, the radical disconnect between sign and meaning becomes evident—most strikingly, and humorously, in the figure of Dogberry.

Deleyto, Celestino. "Men in Leather: Kenneth Branagh's 'Much Ado about Nothing' and Romantic Comedy." *Cinema Journal* 36 (1997): 91-105.

Deleyto uses Kenneth Branagh's *Much Ado about Nothing* (1993) to reflect upon the limits of representing romantic love in contemporary cinema. He argues that Branagh's film shows how in the 1990s a more egalitarian representation of heterosexual love is possible, but that less conventional forms of romance—homosexual and/or interracial—remain marginalized.

Friedman, Michael D. "Male Bonds and Marriage in *All's Well* and *Much Ado*." *Studies in English Literature* 35 (1995): 231-249.

Friedman compares Claudio to Bertram in *All's Well that Ends Well*, showing how 20th-century productions have attempted to find ways to make these problematic characters redeemable.

Garber, Marjorie. "*Much Ado About Nothing*." In *Shakespeare After All*. New York: Pantheon, 2004.

Garber offers a comprehensive (and extremely readable) introduction to the major issues of the play, following in particular the multiple meanings of "nothing/noting" throughout the text.

Howard, Jean E. "Renaissance antitheatricality and the politics of gender and rank in *Much Ado About Nothing*." In *Shakespeare Reproduced: The text in history and ideology*. Jean E. Howard and Marion F. O'Connor, eds. New York and London: Routledge, 1987.

Looking at *Much Ado* from feminist and new historicist perspectives, Howard contends that the play not only reveals the patriarchal dynamics that were evident in Shakespeare's day, but that it also served to buttress the prevailing ideologies.

Leggatt, Alexander. "*Much Ado About Nothing*." In *Shakespeare's Comedy of Love*. London: Methuen, 1974.

Leggatt contrasts the rhetorical, artificial quality of the language employed by certain characters in *Much Ado* with the naturalistic speech used by others and illustrates what each says about the prospects of love.

McCollom, William G. "The Role of Wit in *Much Ado About Nothing*." *Shakespeare Quarterly* 19 (1968): 165-174.

Anatomizing the forms of wit that are evident in the play, McCollom illustrates how *Much Ado* juxtaposes false wisdom, which is rooted in deception, with true wit, which teaches humility.

Mueschke, Paul and Miriam Mueschke. "Illusion and Metamorphosis in *Much Ado About Nothing.*" *Shakespeare Quarterly* 18 (1967): 53-65.

Honor is the principal concern in the class-conscious society of *Much Ado*, Paul and Miriam Mueschke argue. Don John, who, as a bastard son, is denied full access to honor, is thus the mainspring of the plot, as his discontent leads the other male characters to disillusionment.

Myhill, Nova. "Spectatorship in/of *Much Ado About Nothing.*" *Studies in English Literature* 39 (1999): 291-311.

Myhill notes that in a play about the problems of observation, the audience in the theater is also positioned as a spectator. Denied direct access to critical scenes—such as the staging of Hero's "infidelity"—the spectators are dependent, like the characters in the play, on the reports of others, thus challenging the assumption that the audience is an omniscient third party, secure from manipulation.

Straznicky, Marta. "Shakespeare and the Government of Comedy: *Much Ado about Nothing.*" *Shakespeare Studies* 22 (1994): 141-171.

Straznicky uses Michel Foucault's work on the ideologies of power to look at the play. She contends that *Much Ado* evinces not only the tension between sovereign and subject, but reveals the remarkably complex matrix of power between individuals.

FILMOGRAPHY

Much Ado About Nothing (1973). Directed by A.J. Antoon. With Sam Waterston (Benedick) and Kathleen Widdoes (Beatrice). 165 Minutes.

    Originally a stage production for the New York Shakespeare Festival directed by Joseph Papp, A. J. Antoon's *Much Ado* is self-consciously American, set in a small town at the conclusion of the Spanish-American War. Filled with inventive stage business, this film is primarily comic, with shades of sentimentality.

Much Ado About Nothing (1984). Directed by Stuart Burge. With Cherie Lunghi (Beatrice), Robert Lindsay (Benedick) and Jon Finch (Don Pedro). 148 Minutes.

    Stuart Burge directed *Much Ado About Nothing* for the BBC's *Complete Dramatic Works of William Shakespeare* series. The acting is superb, highlighting nuances in the main characters that are often blunted in other productions; the language, spoken with clarity and purpose, is the centerpiece of the film.

Much Ado About Nothing (1993) Directed by Kenneth Branagh. With Kenneth Branagh (Benedick), Emma Thompson (Beatrice), Denzel Washington (Don Pedro), Keanu Reeves (Don John) and Michael Keaton (Dogberry). 111 minutes.

    The combination of internationally-recognized stars and experienced stage actors, along with its high production values and gorgeous setting, made Kenneth Branagh's *Much Ado* one of the films that sparked the revival of Shakespearean cinema in the 1990s.

Shakespeare Retold: Much Ado About Nothing (2005). Directed by Brian Percival. With Sarah Parish (Beatrice), Damian Lewis (Benedick), and Billie Piper (Hero). 90 minutes.

    One of a four-part miniseries of modernized Shakespeare plays (along with *Macbeth*, *The Taming of the Shrew*, and *A Midsummer Night's Dream*), this adaptation casts Beatrice and Benedick as anchors on a television news program and brings contemporary sexual politics to the forefront.